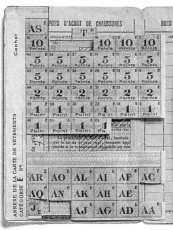

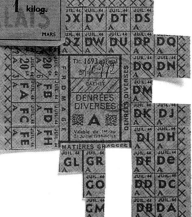

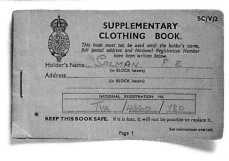

TO NICOLAS

GERARD AND FREDERIC FINEL

REMEMBER
44

TEXT BY CLAUDE FLORY · PHOTOGRAPHS BY DIDIER TRUFFAUT

TRANSLATED FROM FRENCH BY YVES COLEMAN AND DIMITRA PARDALIS

EDITIONS OUEST-FRANCE
13, rue du Breil, Rennes

Day by day, you experience the Second World War in these pages as unknown and ordinary people lived it. Through our characters and the objects that surround them, you will experience a world comprised of tragedy and routine, courage and sometimes humor.

A radio, a poster, a piece of clothing, a sentimental ballad, the smell of a cigarette. It's a moment that will suddenly spring up in your memory. A time that some have not known and others have forgotten.

You were close to these four people or you heard of them, afterwards. John Richardson, the British Squadron Leader, David O'Neill, the American colonel, Jeannot the French maquisard and Geneviève Voisin, a young Parisian woman grappling with the everyday reality of the Occupation.

For four years John Richardson and his men have endured the German bombing of their base located near Canterbury. They return blow for blow. Colonel David O'Neill trains his troops in Massachusetts and bites his nails waiting for D-Day. Jeannot joins the Resistance to escape to the STO (Compulsory Labor Service). He hides on a farm, with some friends of his age. They await the weapons and munitions that London promised to parachute. Armed only with old rifles, they try to organize raids against the Germans and they threaten collaborationists. Jeannot assumes the name D'Artagnan for the duration of the war. Geneviève Voisin stands in line in front of shops to get food for her family. Sometimes she forgets to use a food coupon before it goes out of date. Last time it was an A ticket allowing for the purchase of 350 grams of grape sugar, a substitute to put in a fake coffee. She buys food on the black market to

© Edilarge S.A. Éditions Ouest-France, Rennes, 1994.

improve the everyday fare. Albert, her husband, is liberated from his prisoners Stalag by the "relief": whereby one prisoner is exchanged against three volunteers who will go to work in Germany. Albert does not like the Germans, but he respects Marshal Pétain and does not want to "re-enlist" in the Resistance.

In 1944, all of these people find themselves in liberated France. They are the unwitting actors in a tragic adventure which ends, after five years of struggle and bloodshed, with an overwhelming victory of the Free World over hate and contempt.

As the days go by, John Richardson, David O'Neill, Jeannot and Geneviève are overwhelmed with feelings of helplessness, shame and desire for revenge. They describe their emotions in diaries which now offer a chronicle of those dark years when hope alone made life possible.

We have found the raw material of these diaries hidden deep in the corners of memory, dispersed or forgotten in libraries. Bit by bit, we have shaped them and reconstituted the universe of their authors. These "diaries" are not a fiction, they tell only real facts, but they are not historical documents. Our four imagined characters portray the experience of whole fractions of the French, American and British population.

This universe is furnished with more than two thousand authentic objects chosen for their relevance to and existence in this period. They are the fruits of research by a network of collectors fascinated by this part of history. This book is not an encyclopaedia. It provides the reader a means to know and understand better a time as dramatic and disconcerting as the Second World War. It is a distant part of history which is still very close to us and full of not so distant hopes and sacrifices.

DORYPHORES _ TÊTES DE MORT
Tous les Chleuhs passent
ici. Inquiétant!
Raymond essaie d'identifier
les régiments. D'après
leurs insignes, ce sont
des durs à cuire.

Marcel transmet à
Londres. On va bien savoir
où ils vont. Pas question
de bouger.
Ils sont armés jusqu'aux
dents.
[Attendons les ordres]

"Jerries", "Death's heads", all the "Huns" pass through here. It's upsetting. Raymond keeps trying to identify the regiments. They are hard nuts to crack according to their badges. Marcel informed London. We'll find out where they are going. There's no question of moving. They are armed to the teeth. Let's just await orders.

Service jacket of a German Artillery Sergeant Major (Oberfeldwebel); Panzer officer cap; military record books; P38 pistol case; belt, 98K Mauser bayonet and cartridge pouch; map case; gas mask in standard canister; stick hand grenade.

For the Wehrmacht that has everything...

The German soldiers' uniform provokes the curiosity of occupied France. Accustomed to the varied designs and colors of their own regiments' clothes – from the red cape of the Spahis, the North African riders, and the Algerians' djellabah, to the puttees of the infantrymen –, the French people are surprised by the Wehrmacht's uniforms which seem so simple and utilitarian. They are further impressed by the imposing presence of these handsome blond and sportive soldiers in black leather boots. Each branch of the army uses a different color: green for the infantry, blue-grey for the air force, black for the armored vehicle divisions and dark blue for the navy with two small pieces of ribbon hanging on the back of the cap. Female auxiliaries are dressed entirely in grey, which explains why they are nicknamed the "grey mice." Rank is indicated on the shoulder traps. All that makes the identification much easier for the Resistance fighters. They are able to recognize the enemy forces and regularly inform London about their movements.

Looking for fresh supplies. Saw four photos on the chimney of a farm: Pétain, de Gaulle, Pope Pius XII and Stalin. A shock. The explanation I received: "They are all against Hitler. It's just that they don't say it the same way. It all adds up to the same thing though. Six of one and half-a-dozen of the other, it's all politics. They can't fool us."

The Marshal's sun

Torn between the trust and respect that they feel for the victor of Verdun and their horror of discipline, the broad mass of French people come up with good rationalizations to avoid having to choose between Pétain and de Gaulle. They like to think that a valorous soldier can't be a traitor and a noble general can't be "sold" to the English. Both will con everyone. The French people listen to Radio London at night near the fireside. They demonstrate in the streets to applaud Marshal Pétain. In Lyons, on the 18th and 19th of November 1940, 150,000 persons acclaim the old man. Cardinal Gerlier, archbishop of Lyons, exclaims from his pulpit: "Pétain is France and France is Pétain." In the town of Vienne, during the Spring of 1941, on a sunny day described as a "Marshal's sun," a frenzy of excitement welcomes Pétain.

April 1944, the die is cast. Nevertheless, the "Savior of France" receives an ovation from the crowd assembled in front of Paris's City Hall.

Prominent personalities are decorated with the Francisque, a double-sided axe which is the emblem of the Vichy régime.

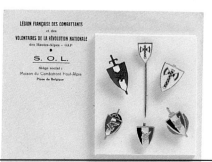

The SOL (para-military organisation) ensures that "good" principles are implemented.

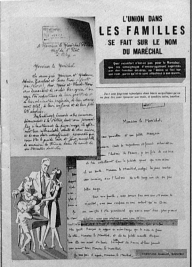

Work – Family – Fatherland, these three watchwords sum up the ideals of the Vichy government and they are completed through Pétain's famous sentence : "Land never lies" which justifies his politics of the "return to the land."

Many sycophants – like René Benjamin, Lucien Rebattet and Abel Bonnard, a member of the French Academy – write books to glorify the "Leader" who often presents himself as the savior of France.

Behind the Barbe

It's him. Here he is. Bearded like a soldier of WWI. At the door of his train car, with his back bent, is Albert. My husband. I was informed yesterday that he was liberated "thanks to the relief." I owe this to four Frenchmen who will take his place and work in German factories. Obviously the Germans got a very good deal, but workers apparently earn a good wage. I selfishly savor his return.

POW's become hostages

The 1,850,000 POW's (prisoners of war) are the chips for bargaining. France is deprived of living forces. The Germans, surprised by their number, don't know what to do with them. First they consider liberating some POW's and a small number take advantage of the confusion and escape. Most POW's, however, think they will be liberated quickly. There are approximately 1.5 million prisoners in the *Frontstalags* of France when the occupying forces realize that prisoners can be used to apply pressure. Then the POW's are transferred to Germany in 14 *Oflags* (for the officers) and 56 *Stalags* (for the privates). Germans use privates as laborers in factories and farms. Living conditions are sometimes hard and dangerous and each escape is punished with sanctions. Despite the substantial efforts of the government to free them or improve their conditions, the French State comes up against a brick wall. The POW's have become hostages.

Photo albums, photographs, drawings, postcard, mess tins on whic soldiers have carved their names; sentimental items constitute memories of captivity.
Below right: a jacket with the prisoner's black triangle.

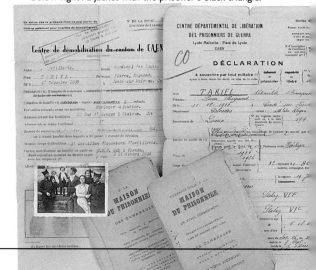

Ce matin, dans "Je suis Partout", il y avait un article incroyable "Ils sont vraiment partis comme partaient pour la première croisade ceux qu'enflammaient la voix des frères prêcheurs et des guerriers illuminés par la foi." C'est signé Brasillach! Il parle du départ pour le front russe du premier contingent de la LVF. Et en plus, le 12 octobre, ils ont prêté serment à Hitler sous l'uniforme allemand!

Read this morning in Je suis partout: "They left like those who took part in the first crusade, impassioned by the voices of preaching friars and warriors illuminated by their faith." Robert Brasillach wrote that! He is talking about the departure of the LVF first contingent for the Russian front. Most revolting: they took the oath of allegiance to Hitler in German uniform on October 12th!

Poor Charlemagne!

"Bolsheviks, Freemasons and Jews" are the three targets of the Vichy régime. These are the enemies of the German Army as well. Those who fight on the Eastern front with the Wehrmacht pretend that they are defending Western civilization. The LVF (Legion of French Volunteers) was born with Hitler's blessing on two conditions: that it should not enroll more than 15,000 soldiers and that it should fight in the uniform of German infantry. Despite a briskly-led advertising campaign, it recruits only 4,000 soldiers and 113 officers. In 1942, the LVF is decimated near Moscow by Russian partisans. The Germans prefer to recruit for the Waffen SS, a surer, more carefully controlled force. They create the Charlemagne Division. In 1945, its remnants would defend the Führer's bunker in Berlin.

LÉGION DES VOLONTAIRES FRANÇA[IS]
Contre le Bolchevisme

CONDITIONS D'ENGAGEMENT

1° Les engagements au titre de l'Infanterie et de l'Artillerie sont seuls acceptés.
Peuvent être admis:
a) Les anciens militaires ayant servi dans toutes les autres armes.
b) Les jeunes gens, âgés de plus de dix-neuf ans, n'ayant jamais été soldat, porteur d'une autorisati[on] paternelle légalisée.

2° Être Aryen, Français ou avoir servi à titre Français. N'avoir encouru aucune condamnation infamante.

SOLDES ET AVANTAGES

GRADES	En première ligne célibat.	maries
Soldat	2.400	3.000
Caporal	2.820	3.423
Sergent	3.540	4.340
Sergent-Chef et Sergent-Major	4.100	5.200
Adjudant	4.480	5.780
Adjudant-Chef et Aspirant	4.700	6.000

Allocation familiale: 360 francs par mois et par enfant au-dessous de 16 ans. — Logement, habillement soigné, bonne nourriture, tabac journalier, le tout à titre gratuit. — Familles aidées et suivies pendant l'absence. — Permission de détente.

CAMARADE,

La France est ton pays... La **Waffen SS** française lutte non pour l'Allemagne, mais pour ta Patrie... pour une Europe libre, unie et réconciliée !...

DEMANDE D'ENGAGEMENT

Les volontaires désirant s'engager dans la Waffen SS s'adressent à un des bureaux de renseignements mentionnés ci-dessous :

LILLE, 14, rue Faidherbe.
DOUAI, 9, rue de Bellain.
LENS, 36, rue de la Paix.
ROUBAIX, 3, Grande Rue.
TOURCOING, Grand' Place.
CALAIS, 3, Boulev. La Fayette.

Ces bureaux sont ouverts chaque jour de 8 h. 30 à 19 h. 30 sans interruption.
Le dimanche ces bureaux sont ouverts de 8 h. 30 à 13 h.
Le départ des volontaires a lieu immédiatement ou à une date choisie par le volontaire.
Un large soutien aussi bien matériel que pécuniaire est assuré aux familles des volontaires.

☛ Renseignements complémentaires dans les bureaux de recrutement susnommés.

Jeune Fille Française

Veux-tu préparer la révolution sociale ?
Veux-tu être forte, saine, sportive ?
Veux-tu donner une nouvelle race à la France ?
Veux-tu suivre le maréchal PÉTAIN ?
Aujourd'hui tu soulageras la misère.
Demain tu construiras un foyer.

Si tu t'en sens capable, viens aux

JEUNESSES POPULAIRES FRANÇAISES

Président d'honneur : Jacques Doriot
3, rue Cimarosa, PARIS (16°)

CAHIERS de L'ÉMANCIPATION NATIONALE

MARCEL DÉAT

Perspectives françaises

nder a Strange Cross

Propaganda is omnipresent on walls and in bookshop windows : enlistment posters for the Legion of French Volunteers and for Jacques Doriot's French Patriotic Youths ; pseudo-intellectual, ridiculous and agressive pamphlets ; anti-British and anti-semitic literature. All this under the watchful leadership of the *Milice* whose emblem is a gamma, the sign of Aries and a symbol of strength and renewal.

> *De retour de Dourdan, je suis montée dans le compartiment avec deux énormes valises bourrées de ravitaillement.*
>
> *Arrivée à la gare d'Orsay, comme tous les dimanche soirs, sévères contrôles.*
>
> *Tous les trois pas, je pose mes bagages sur le quai en soufflant. Un militaire allemand me sourit. Il emporte les valises. Et hop, on passe !*

Back from Dourdan. Got on the train with two huge suitcases stuffed with food. There were strict controls at Orsay station as on every Sunday night. Every three steps I put my luggage down on the platform and puffed. A German soldier smiled at me, took my suitcases and hup! we went through the checkpoint.

When you leave your house, you better have all the necessary papers with you in order to avoid being arrested by the Gendarmerie, the *Milice* or the Gestapo.

A man without papers is a dead man

During these terrible years, a man without papers is a dead man. There are plenty of forms. To cross the demarcation line, one needs an authorization which must be obtained from the *Kommandantur* a long time in advance. For certain zones, a special pass is required. Only Admiral Darlan, when he was chief of Cabinet, had a permanent *Ausweis* (permit). Still, to travel is a question of habit. Crossing the demarcation line is an important network of more or less trustworthy and efficient smugglers. For a fee they help people pass in and out of the occupied zone. Anything can be bought, but those who want to travel must be prepared with cash. Controls are strict. More and more tricks are necessary to slip through the security net.

London in Dinne

Marvellous evening at Edward Stirling's. Two air raids, apparently. Bombs are noisy things. They oblige us to raise our voices. How annoying!
Received a phone call: "Sorry dear, there's a big hole outside the front door; a bomb. You'll have to come in through the window. We're dressing for dinner of course, as usual."

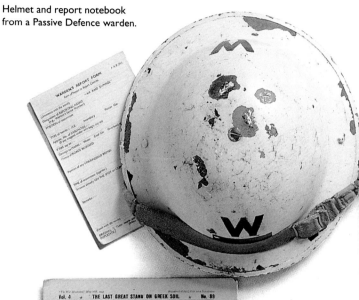

Helmet and report notebook from a Passive Defence warden.

A season in Hell

There are incendiary and explosive bombs, and mines on small parachutes which explode on the ground. A deluge of metal and fire pummels London.

It's the 15th of September 1940. A thousand bombers take off from the French coasts protected by the fighters. They are marked with the black cross, the painted badge of the Luftwaffe planes. They drop their bombs on military targets in preparation for an invasion of England. The Royal Air Force moves to check the offensive, and in retaliation to this unexpected resistance, the Germans begin attacking civilians and bombing towns. The Blitz lasts eight months. At night, Londoners take refuge in the tube stations. During the day they attend to their affairs as if nothing were happening. With a composure peculiar to British people, they pass the craters dug by bombs without even glancing at them. Complete indifference!

German firebomb.
Armbands for volunteer firemen.

acket during the Blitz

struction handbooks
air raids, Air Raid
otection armband
d badge.

GAS ATTACK

OFFICIAL INSTRUCTIONS ISSUED BY THE MINISTRY OF HOME SECURITY

HOW TO PUT ON YOUR GAS MASK

Always keep yo
gas mask
— day a

PACKING OF RESPIRATOR.

THE PROTECTION OF YOUR HOME AGAINST AIR RAIDS

HOME OFFICE

READ THIS BOOK THROUGH THEM KEEP IT CAREFULLY

1. Hold your breath. Put on mask wherever you are. Close window.

2. If out of doors, take off hat, put on your mask. Turn up collar.

3. Put on gloves or keep hands in pockets. Take cover in nearest building.

ARP

IF YOU GET GASSED

BY VAPOUR GAS

Keep your gas mask on even if you feel discomfort
If discomfort continues go to First Aid Post

3 If you can't get Ointment or Cream within

4 Take of

LOOK OUT IN THE BLACK-OUT

Civilian gas mask for baby.

"Scramble"! The crew's already through the door, for the third time this morning. Messerschmidts sighted. Three minutes to take off. I'm wearing my "Mae-West" life jacket in case we come down in the drink... and a parachute of course. Broke the record for speed: 2'30", ignition chocks, maybe I'll bag a "Jerry."

Wooden instruction models for pilots; above, the German Messerschmitt 210; below, the American Lockheed P38.

Instruction handbook for Royal Air Force pilots.

The deadly ballet of the knights of the sky

With 900 flights through the London sky, Royal Air Force fighters win the Battle of Britain on the 15th of September 1940. On alert day and night, the pilots in their Hurricanes and Spitfires shoot down 185 enemy planes. They lose 26 planes and 13 men are missing in action. German fighters are confronted by three main obstacles: the radar networks that they have neglected to destroy; the anti-aircraft guns; and the blimps (nicknamed the "sausages"), which are solidly fixed to the ground with a thick cable and make imposing barriers. As a result, the ME109s are obliged to tack and burn a lot of fuel; they have a mere ten minutes of autonomy above London to protect the bombers that they are escorting. They are easily preyed upon by Allied fighters. The Luftwaffe is increasingly obliged to give up in the face of these murderous raids.

The Engines are Ticking Over

This is the *Who's Who* for the Battle of Britain. For only 3 guineas, the *Daily Mirror* offers its readers a guide to the sky : who is flying up there, friend or foe?

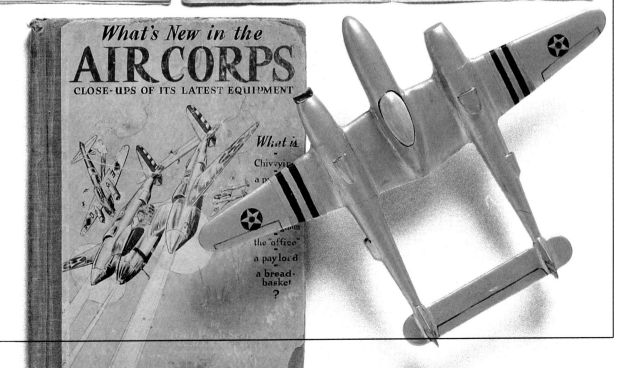

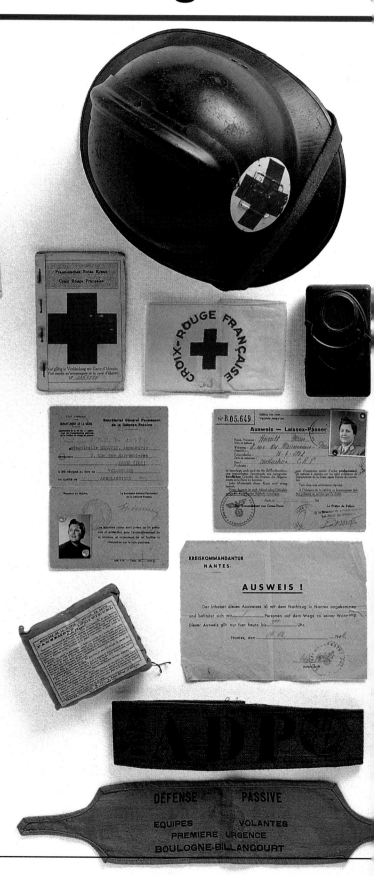

Croisième alerte cette nuit. Cette fois c'est pour nous. Fusées éclairantes, bandes d'alu qui scintillent sous les projecteurs. La vague suivante arrive déjà.

La DCA claque. Les éclats d'obus tombent dans la cour. D'un coup ça siffle et ça explose. C'était pas loin!

Après deux heures de ce régime, on a plus envie de dormir, alors, on fait un monopoly jusqu'au petit matin.

The third alert tonight, and this time it's for us. There are flares, aluminium strips which sparkle under the anti-aircraft lights. The next wave is already coming and the anti-aircraft defense is ringing out. Pieces of shrapnel are falling in the courtyard. There was just a hiss and explosion, not too far away. Two more hours like this, and there is no way we'll be able to sleep tonight. We'll play Monopoly till dawn.

Bombs don't destroy in detail

A descent into the shelters is a descent into Hell. Despite the efforts of block leaders and members of the Passive Defence, people are reluctant to go into the shelters. The French people are getting used to bombings. In 1944, air-raid sirens drag them out of their beds several times each night. It is a show, like a fireworks display on a national holiday. Everyone dreams about the end of the war. Horrible stories circulate about people buried alive or drowned in bomb shelters after water pipes burst. People prefer to die in the open air. Blind in the face of the danger? No doubt. People living in Normandy are in a position to know. They are on a permanent alert. At the request of the Allies who send leaflets over the whole region, they flee from their houses to take refuge in the woods. Smoking ruins and the smell of corpses do not put off volunteers who clear away the debris. Sixty-seven thousand French civilians die under the bombs of their liberators.

Fire, Steel and Blood

For a long time, the French
government took every
precaution to protect
the population against
bombings. In 1940,
French people expecting
German bombers find that
Allied planes drop bombs on their
country instead. Initially frightened,
the population becomes increasingly curious.
"Chaffs," aluminium stripes intended to fool radar,
sparkle in the light from anti-aircraft spots.
The chaffs, along with flares, offer Parisians a true show.

Hier, j'ai vu une affiche sur les murs de Paris. Par arrêté préfectoral: "Il est interdit de jeter, brûler, détruire, sauf cas de salubrité publique, les déchets et vieilles matières tels que vieux chiffons, ferrailles, vieux métaux, vieux papiers, plumes, caoutchouc, os, peaux, crins". Et une deuxième annonce la récupération des "cornes, onglons et sabots".

Je me demande ce qu'on peut en faire! De toute façon, nous n'aurons bientôt plus rien à jeter!

Posters recently mounted in the city announce two new laws issued by the prefect. Except where public safety is in question, it is forbidden to throw away, burn or destroy any rubbish or materials including rags, scraps, metals, papers, feathers, rubber, bones, leather and horsehair. The second law requires recycling the "horns and hooves of pigs, cows and horses." I wonder what can be done with all that. Anyway, soon we won't have anything left to throw away.

Butts are a big hit

Everyone recycles. The Germans reuse statues by melting the bronze to make guns. The French recycle used objects, even packages and wrappings. One is often obliged to return them in exchange for whatever product one wants to buy. Even clipped metro tickets are reprocessed. Hard times inspire the imagination of inventors and handymen alike. A true *Concours Lépine*. An engineer sensitive to the cold uses newspaper to insulate his bedroom. Another substitutes coal with nuggets of newspaper fabricated by a home-made press. A small plastic tube becomes a pumping device making the use of a stove possible when there is almost no pressure left in the pipes. The most inventive example of recycling must be cigarette butts that are carefully stocked in a waterproof iron box. When the box is full, the remaining bits of tobacco are removed from the original paper and re-rolled into new cigarettes.

Let Imagination Take Power

...othing is wasted, everything is patched up.

ATTENTION !
économisez le GAZ

This gas pumping device compensates for the lack of pressure in the gas pipes.

People experiment with many uses for paper, such as fuel (paper pellets for stoves), as well as for making strings, bags, etc.

...ortage reigns. Locksmiths discover that they can make ...ys with aluminium. Electricians remember that wood was ...e first material used for insulation.

Almanach de la Famille française
1941

Foyer de France

ALMANACH DE LA FAMILLE FRANÇAISE

1943

1943   ALMANACH des Postes, Télégraphes et Téléphones   1943

1943

1942

Escalope: de Rutabaga

Denrées nécessaires:

- Un gros rutabaga,
- poivre, sel,
- lait écrémé et chapelure

Couper en tranches
le rutabaga pelé.

Donner à vos tranches
la forme d'une escalope de veau.

Plonger dans l'eau bouillante.
Sécher et saupoudrer de
poivre et de sel.
Panner dans une chapelure au lait.

Rôtir dans la graisse.

Escalopes of rutabaga. Ingredients: one big rutabaga, pepper, salt, skimmed milk and dried bread-crumbs. Peel and slice the rutabaga into shapes like a veal escalope. Plunge the slices into boiling water. Remove, pat dry and sprinkle with pepper and salt. Coat each piece with bread-crumbs mixed with milk. Fry until crisp.

Tomatoes in gardens and rabbits on balconies

The rationing of the French population – provoked by the lack of imports, the drain of occupying forces and the purchases of various German *Büros* – encourages resourcefulness. There are eight kinds of ration cards for food, clothes, and tobacco. E, J1 and J2 cards go to children. The J3 are for those between 13 and 21 years. Adults receive A cards. Old people receive V cards. T and C cards are allotted to forced labourers and farm workers. People fight to obtain the T card because it allows for slightly larger rations. The system works through tickets, lettered coupons. One must keep up with the newspapers to know when to use them and one needs to register with shopkeepers. Fraud reigns: fake cards, black market, "agricultural" parcels sent from cousins living in the countryside and violent raids of farms. Tomatoes grow in the Tuileries gardens and rabbits are reared on balconies.

the Means

Panets (a variety of turnip), rutabagas and Jerusalem artichokes; previously neglected, these vegetables are used in all sorts of recipes. The "Wonder Product" is a fat-free camembert.

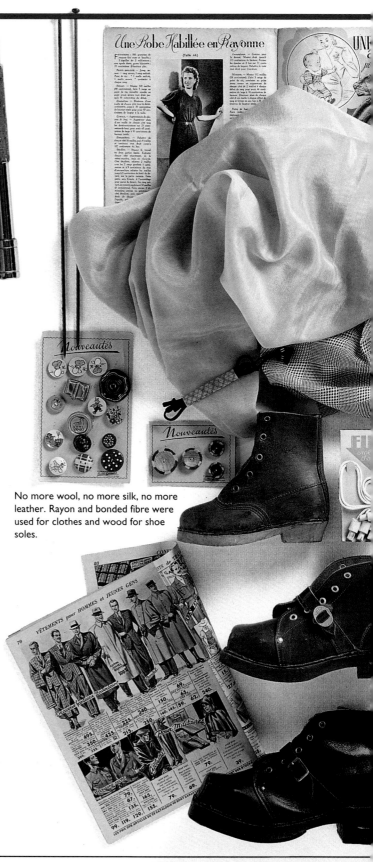

Les autorités elles-mêmes le reconnaissent :
" Avec le contingent de points textiles accordé, il faut 15 ans à la population adulte pour obtenir une robe, un manteau, un complet ou un pardessus. Étant bien entendu que ces calculs excluent l'attribution de toute autre pièce d'habillement ..."

Il va en falloir des astuces pour rester coquette --- et surtout pour empêcher les enfants de grandir !!

"Given the allotted share of textile points, it would take fifteen years for an adult to get a dress, a jacket, a suit or an overcoat, let alone any other piece of clothing..." Even the authorities know this. How many tricks will I have to use to remain attractive and, above all, to keep my children from growing too fast ?

The shortage style

French people can't buy new clothes, they convert their existing wardrobe instead. They transform coats into jackets, shorten their skirts, and darn their socks. Short hair, short skirts, platform shoes : that is fashion in the time of shortage. From time to time, one can get new clothes from shopkeepers by donating used ones to the Secours National. The "national shoes" have a rigid or articulated wooden sole. Fashionable women make up for everything, however, with their hats, which are true monuments perched and balanced on their heads. Head pieces abound in gauze, tulle and verdure. Although the Germans would like to impose their fashion on Europe, high fashion designers continue to create with ingenuity. French men and women dress with studied elegance. The "clic-clac" of wooden soles on the cobblestone is the only sign that times have changed.

No more wool, no more silk, no more leather. Rayon and bonded fibre were used for clothes and wood for shoe soles.

Hatters

lish Frenchwomen do not give
o the shortage, however, and use
essories to revitalize their pre-war
rdrobe. Just a string can become
ag or a belt.

J'ai filé plusieurs mailles de ma dernière paire de bas d'avant-guerre. La remailleuse ne peut plus les réparer. Pas questions de sortir sans! J'ai vu une réclame pour un produit: Filpas. On le passe sur les jambes avec un pinceau et ça les teinte.

"La soie sur vos jambes sans bas de soie" affirme le fabricant! On en trouve dans les grands magasins à 25F seulement!

I have several runs in my last pair of stockings from before the war. The darner can't repair them anymore. I can't go out without them! I saw an ad for a product called Filpas. You paint it on your legs with a brush and it dyes them. It's selling in department stores for 25 francs. "Silk on your legs without silk stockings," the manufacturer says.

The miracle of antibiotics

In the first emergency kit for American soldiers there is Penicillin and Streptomycin. The first antibiotics save thousands of wounded soldiers. These excellent discoveries, made during the war, suddenly transform the life of all sick people. Hygiene products and fashion accessories are in short supply. Only perfumes are not submitted to a quota policy: Guerlain, Houbigant, Schiapparelli and Paquin continue their production. Still, the prices are so high that they become exceptional products. Soap – real soap – is extremely rare. Numerous replacements are produced with alkali, slaked lime and lichen. At best they make no lather. At worst they damage skin already affected by winter chilblains. A poster advertises soap or a pack of washing powder in exchange for a kilo of bones.

Penicillin !

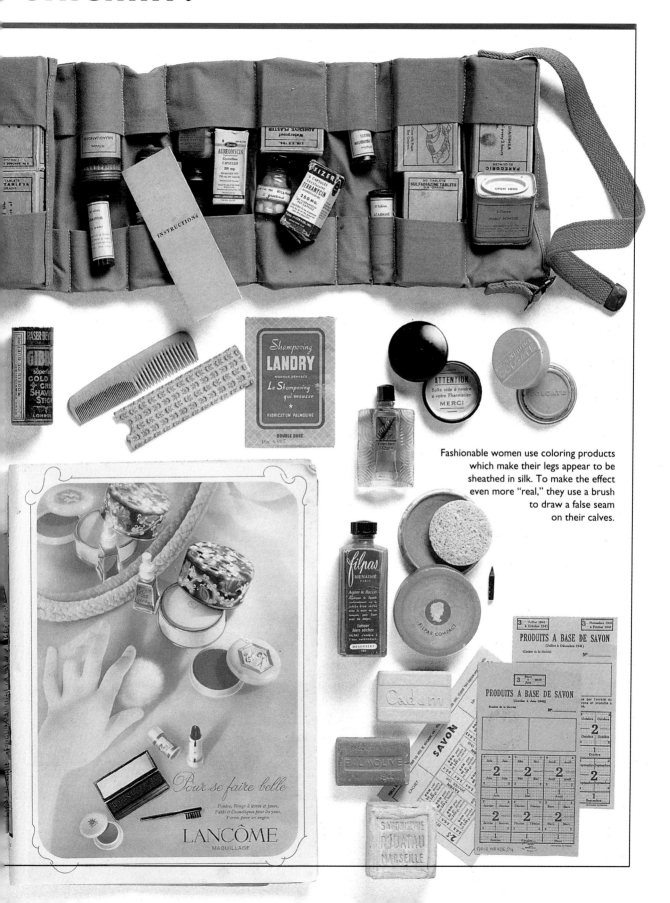

Fashionable women use coloring products which make their legs appear to be sheathed in silk. To make the effect even more "real," they use a brush to draw a false seam on their calves.

Le "Petit Parisien" raconte que des Collabos, armés, de ciseaux ont corrigé et tondu des jeunes. Des zazous. Ces garçons et ces filles, qu'on voit un peu partout. Ils s'habillent long malgré la pénurie. Ils traînent leur désœuvrement dans les Cafés et écoutent du Jazz. Une grande offensive s'annonce contre eux.

The Petit Parisien reports that collaborators, armed with scissors, roughed and sheared some Zazous. These boys and girls can be seen everywhere these days. Zazous dress long despite the shortage. Idle, they hang around in cafés and listen to jazz. A big campaign against them is on its way.

Charm and shock : Chevalier, Piaf, Trenet

For boys : a long jacket, short, tight trousers, four-sole shoes, wavy hair and a rolled umbrella. For girls : a wool, turtleneck sweater, a very short pleated skirt, long hair, striped stockings and flat shoes. That's the *zazou* look.

They rebel through their eccentric fashion. They listen to jazz and jump around in dance halls and discos to the sound of *Je suis swing*, Johnny Hess's 1939 tune.

Rivaling jazz fashion in importance is the craze over accordion music and light-hearted songs. Charles Trenet, Edith Piaf and Maurice Chevalier enjoy a huge success. So do Léo Marjane, Suzy Solidor, Tino Rossi and Lina Margy with the song : *Le petit vin blanc*.

This movement will lead to the triumph of jazz in Saint-Germain-des-Prés after the *Plum-plum Tralala* of 1945 and the "cowboy" songs of Yves Montand.

Zazou, Zazou

Suzanne and her children are here until tomorrow. We are trying to prepare the nicest Christmas possible with what we have. Hopefully I still have the box of garlands and Christmas decorations, and I have made a little Christmas tree out of paper. What luck to be all together! We will keep in mind all the children whose fathers are still held prisoner in Germany.

Picoulet, the pilot, a[...]
3 laughing *maquisar[...]*
make funny fac[...]
at the occupyi[...]
force[...]

An orange for Christmas!

Curfew gives politics a hand

After Work and before Fatherland, Family is the second element of the Vichy régime's motto. Propaganda does not let an opportunity pass by without sanctifying mothers, especially those with many children. There is Mothers' Day, Mothers' Holiday...

People are still trying to find reasons for the 1940 defeat. Marshal Pétain makes his diagnosis public: "Not enough children, not enough weapons, not enough allies." Because the government can't deal with the last two causes for the moment, it decides to focus on the first one. The birth gap is a well known phenomenon. In 1940, there are 200,000 more deaths than births. The government takes some measures and hopes that they will be effective: food benefits, premiums for the first child, single income allowances, various tax exemptions. In 1943, births outnumber deaths by one thousand in spite of the difficult times. But is politics the real reason? Some jokers claim that the curfew is responsible!

All the Children Gone?

here are two coveted treasures : a toy plane reproduction of Mermoz's *Arc-en-ciel*, and a doll named Reuette.

The fleur-de-lys replaces Baden Powell's clover on the buckle and badge of French Scouts. This is the beginning of the famous collection *Signes de piste*.

A leaflet found by Roger at the University:
"French student
November 11th remains
a national holiday for you.
Despite the order of oppressing authorities,
it will be a day of reverence.
You will not attend any classes.
You will honor the Unknown Soldier at 5.30 P.M.
November 11th, 1918 was the day of a great victory.
November 11th, 1940 will signal an even greater one.
All students must stand together -
long live France."

Youth join us!

Youth movements have undergone unprecedented expansion in the free zone as well as in the occupied one. Both sides consciously strive to fashion "men." In Vichy, Youths of the Marshal, Youth Workcamps, and Journeyman's Movement advocate a youth "pure in thoughts, word and deed", thanks to the mythical charisma of Pétain, the victor of Verdun. Youth Day, organized on the 12th of July 1942 in the free zone, is an enormous success. The veteran of youth movements, scouting, is torn apart. On one side of the demarcation line, the Scouts form a line for the Marshal. On the other side, banned, Scouts carry on their activities clandestinely. Students are the first to go into action against the Vichy régime. On the 11th of November 1940 they assemble at the Arc de triomphe. When the Germans shoot, several demonstrators are wounded.

Marshal Pétain

Marshal Pétain is proposed as a model for adults as well as for children. Developing a myth around the victor of Verdun, the Vichy régime establishes a cult of personality. Each action and word from the chief of the French State becomes the object of unlimited admiration. *There was once a Marshal of France* recounts Marshal Pétain's biography with supposedly convincing images and texts. These reassuring images do not stand up to history.

One hundred franc vouchers give ten days of rest to deprived children.

"Here we are before you, Marshal, the Savior of France..." In all the schools, students must sing this refrain which enters into posterity. Some teachers organize a little ceremony to raise the national flag. Others refuse to accept such requirements.

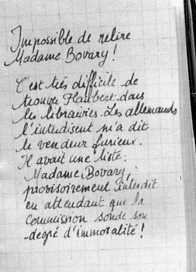

It's impossible to reread Madame Bovary. *The book disappeared from my collection, and it is very difficult to find Flaubert in the bookshops. "The Germans forbid this writer," the bookseller said. He waved a list furiously and read, "Madame Bovary, temporarily banned while the Commission checks its degree of immorality!"*

Shredded literature

Despite insuperable difficulties, people never read as much as during the Occupation. Paper is rare and of poor quality and censorship is merciless. A manuscript needs the stamp of the German *Propagandastaffel* in order to be printed. The "Otto list", a document of 26 four-column pages, is drawn up as early as September 1940 by the occupying forces and revised in 1942 and 1943. It inventories one thousand forbidden books, including Hitler's *Mein Kampf* which is not considered appropriate for the French people. The complete works of 700 Jewish authors are pulped; 2,242 tons of books are destroyed this way. Consequently, second-hand booksellers are given a boost and bookshops make small fortunes. The detective novel, free from any political suspicion, enters its golden era. The number of books borrowed from libraries climbs from 1.2 million in 1939 to 3 million in 1944.

without Books

Je suis allée au cinéma hier soir, voir "Pontcarral, colonel d'Empire" de Jean Delannoy, avec Pierre Blanchard. Je l'adore! Un film patriote! À un moment, Pontcarral-Blanchard dit au juge d'instruction : "Sous un tel régime, Monsieur, c'est un honneur d'être condamné!" Tonnerre d'applaudissements, les gens trépignaient. La direction nous a mis en garde contre ce genre de manifestation...

Some artists refuse to work under the control of the occupying forces. Some go into exile. Others fight in the Free French Forces. Most consider art and politics as two very distinct fields and continue to use their talent to please a public eager for entertainment.

Went to the movies yesterday night. Saw Pontcarral, Colonel of the Empire *by Jean Delannoy with Pierre Blanchar. I adored it. A patriotic movie. At one point Pontcarral says to the committing magistrate : "Under such a political régime, Sir, it's an honor to be condemned!" Thunderous applause followed and the public stamped their feet. The theater's manager warns against this kind of demonstration.*

The first "new wave"

Perhaps because it has recently been recognized as an art, French cinema experiences unprecedented growth. Nevertheless, difficulties of all kinds have never been as prevalent. Two hundred and twenty-five films and 400 one-reelers and cartoons are produced during the war years (compared to 75 films in 1939), despite the imposition of German cinema on Europe, and the censorship and blacklisting of many authors and actors. What films, what actors, what directors! Henri-Georges Clouzot, Jacques Becker, André Cayatte, Claude Autant-Lara. Jean Marais, François Périer, Bernard Blier, Alain Cuny, Gérard Philipe. Jacques Prévert, Marcel Carné. Jean Giraudoux is starting his career as a dialogist in *La Duchesse de Langeais*. Films have prestigious titles : *The Devil's Envoys*, *The Eternal Return* and *Children of Paradise*. It is impossible to forget the scandal created by *The Raven*, whose director, H.-G. Clouzot, is accused of serving German propaganda.

Yet another constraint : to achieve
by force what cannot be obtained
by persuasion, the Germans decide that,
henceforth, all filming must be done in
the German format (16mm). The French
format (17.5 mm) is forbidden.

Il a fallu trois représenta-tions pour voir en entier Cyrano de Bergerac à la Comédie-Française, à cause des alertes. La première fois, descente aux abris pendant la tirade du nez. La deuxième, sirènes dans la pâtisserie de Ragueneau. La fin hier soir... trois mois après! Pour nous punir d'on ne sait quoi, les allemands ont ajourné plusieurs fois la représentation. A cause du couvre-feu, la soirée a commencé à 17 heures.

It took me three performances to see all of Cyrano de Bergerac at the Comédie-Française because of the alerts. The first time, I left for the bomb shelters during the nose monologue. The second time, the air-raid sirens sounded during Ragueneau's pastry. I finally saw the end yesterday evening... three months later! To punish us for I don't know what sin, the Germans repeatedly postponed the performance. Because of the curfew, the show started at 5 P.M.

The show must go on

Cultural life is never interrupted in France – or if so, only briefly. Following the Paris Opera – with Serge Lifar as ballet master –, the Comédie-Française reopens on the 8th of September 1940. Theaters resume their performances quickly. They play Sacha Guitry, Jean-Paul Sartre, Jean Cocteau, Jean Anouilh and Paul Claudel. New plays appear like *The J3*, directed by Roger Ferdinand. It is a comedy of manners about youth under the Occupation. Authors, musicians, actors and cabaret singers are never out of work. Music and dance fascinate the French. Future stars like Roland Petit and Zizi Jeanmaire mature in the shadows. During his captivity, Olivier Messiaen writes *Quatuor pour la fin du temps*.

Some anti-semitic and profascist writers don't hesitate to advocate hate and violence.

for Culture

e length of the Paris Opera grams grows shorter each season, the Parisians' appetite for art ws. Concerts attract bigger and er audiences.

Midday at Périgord Square, 500 yards from the Père-Lachaise cemetery. Saw Calvo, a friend who is drawing a comic strip with animals in the utmost secrecy. The story is about the misfortunes of a crazy dictator named "The Big Bad Wolf" and the text is in captions. Drawing beside him, a 15-year old boy is practising hasty sketches on a piece of paper. Little Uderzo is full of promise.

Stories for 16 and under

Marshal Pétain places blame for the 1940 defeat upon that part of the population that he claims selfishly ignored, and even sabotaged, efforts to protect France. Having given up on the adults, the Vichy government turns to the youth. The youth must be clear-headed, straight and marching in quick time towards the "National Revolution"… just like the victors do.

New children's magazines appear unsullied by the vices of earlier magazines, tricks and lies. They prepare a generation of "good Frenchmen." Their favorite slogan is "Work, Family, Fatherland." They promise a historical Europe, delivered from profiteers. In silence and obscurity, others struggle so that the same youth knows that there exist different paths to renewal. All prepare "Tomorrow's Europe" in their own way.

s Not Dead

The newspapers designed for "modern youth," "conceived and written by Frenchmen," tell of exciting adventures. The propaganda of the Vichy régime targets youth 6 to 12 years, preaching its "good word" to them.

Calvo begins to draw *The Beast is Dead* in 1941. It recounts the story of a big bad wolf (Hitler) who, helped by a pig (Goebbels), tries to seduce a white bear (Stalin) to fight againt a big dog (Churchill). Walt Disney demands modification of the drawings that he finds too similar to his own.

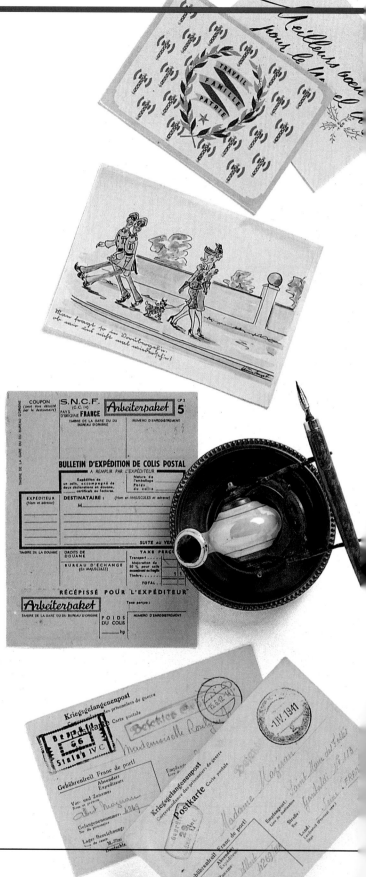

Sent my first interzone postcard to my mother. For twelve lines all I could do was delete inappropriate information. Short to communicate my love and hide my anxiety!

Forbidden communications

Severed into two parts by the iron curtain of the demarcation line after the 25th of June 1940, France's family tree is suddenly uprooted and communication is impossible. Dispersed families, prisoners, people dying on the battlefied and on the roads of the Exodus; everybody is worried about the fate of their family. In September, four months after the country's defeat, "family" postcards are authorized by the occupying forces. Text is reduced to its simplest expression. One needs only "delete as appropriate." In May 1941, the Vichy government replaces these first with postcards allowing for seven original lines of text and then with ordinary postcards. Only in March 1943, a good while after the invasion of the free zone, is it possible to write normally throughout the French territory. People are careful anyway. They know that letters are frequently opened by censors.

Pétainist greeting card for the New Year; German army postcard; dispatch note for a parcel sent to French workers in Germany; French POW mail; pre-stamped postcard with control stamp; stamps bearing an effigy of the Legion of French Volunteers in the Wehrmacht; album of Free France stamps; microfilm messages used by the American army; British soldier postcards; envelopes from the Belgian Bank exiled in London.

Two new fighting men have made front page news: Doctor Carrot and Potato Pete - odd looking chaps! The Ministry of Supplies has created these fictitious characters for children - what a curious initiative! Apparently they are fighting to win the war - the war of vitamins, that is! They are doing it along with Churchill and King George V. I understand, of course, but even so.....

The "War Production" logo can be found on men's shirts and silk stockings.

For King and Country!

Since the beginning of the war, resupplying has been an essential preoccupation of the British Government. The country is subjected to severe rationing through a ticket system more or less similar to the one functioning in France. If England lacks numerous products, it is spared the drain suffered by occupied countries. The black market is virtually non-existent. The English display their legendary public spirit. Fifty-five per cent of the population is drafted in the army or works for the war industries. Women serve in anti-aircraft defense, drive ambulances and farm with tractors. Cultivated lands have increased by 50 percent. The prices of essential products are controlled and quantities are measured. The consumption of food has dropped by 20 percent, but meat and bread products are never rationed.

The basic weekly ration for two adults in summer 1943: 2 mutton chops, 200g of bacon, 50g of cheese, 400g of lard, 150g of chocolate, 200g of jam, 200g of sugar, 50g of powdered egg, 5 pints of milk.

Met an ace RAF pilot. He was just back from a mission over France. During the raid, he made ten passes over the target in order to drop his bombs accurately. On his way home the flak and the fighters got on his tail and tried to shoot him down. Not a scratch. He's only 28 and already a Group Captain with a DSO.

Right on target

Among all Allied pilots sent to bomb France every day from 1943 onward, the English ones are most famous. (French pilots are never sent to bomb their own country.) The British don't drop their bombs just any-where and many of them never return to their base because they spare the civilian population at all costs. They try especially hard not to bomb densely populated districts and, when their planes are badly damaged, pilots prefer to drown in a river or crash into a field rather than fall onto a block of buildings while on fire. During the raid of March 3rd, 1943 on the Renault plants in Paris, crews are ordered to return with their bombs rather than to get rid of them by dropping them anywhere. They risk getting shot down by German fighters awaiting them on their return. Their weight and the nature of their cargo make them more vulnerable. The British government does not hesitate to reward the exploits of these young pilots by nominating them to high ranks remarkable for their youth.

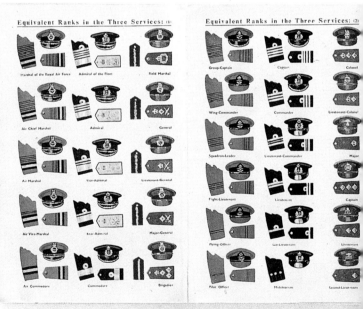

1. General; 2. General cap insignia; 3. Brigadier; 4. Warrant Officer 1st class;
5. Regimental Quartermaster Sergeant; 6. Warrant Officer, 2nd class;
7. Major-general; 8. Brigadier; 9. Colonel; 10. Lieutenant-colonel; 11. Major;
12. Captain; 13. Lieutenant; 14. 2nd Lieutenant; 15. Service chevrons;
16. Colour Sergeant; 17. Sergeant; 18. Corporal; 19. Lance Corporal;
20. Instruction handbooks with identification reviews of different ranks;
21. Combat jacket 40 Pattern of a lance corporal from the Royal
Northumberland Fusiliers, 11th Armored Division.

Colonel

7

8

9

10

11

12

13

14

15

16

17

18

19

20

21

RANK AND BADGES
IN THE
NAVY, ARMY, R·A·F
AND AUXILIARIES

A fully coloured guide to
the badges worn by
members of
His Majesty's Forces

Edited by
E. C. TALBOT-BOOTH
Paymr. Lieut.-Commander, R.N.R.

LONDON
GEORGE PHILIP & SON, LTD., 32 FLEET STREET, E.C.
LIVERPOOL: PHILIP, SON & NEPHEW, LTD., 50 CHURCH STREET

PRINTED IN GREAT BRITAIN

R. NORTHUMBERLAND FUS.

The only comforting thing about this war is that the British have always been able to assert their superiority everywhere. Some one told me an astonishing anecdote about D-day. A commando bagpiper, up to his waist in water, played "Highland Laddie" under a rain of mortar shells and a hail of bullets. Not in the least surprised, his comrades marched past him and on to the slaughter.

Singing in the bullets

Never in their history have the British accepted renouncing a single tradition. During glorious days as well as gloomy ones, they remain faithful to themselves with the same stubbornness, the same phlegm and the same hatred for the petty criticisms of others. Their attitude is particularly conspicuous in the army. Their regiments have kept their original names : Welsh Guards, Irish Guards, Royal Norfolk, Black Watch – even though they fight with rockets and tanks. On parade, they march past with caps, musical instruments and their mascot as if they are afraid that their personality will melt into the same khaki universe as the rest of the world. They don't hesitate to face death with nobility and gallantry. Still, they know that the time has come to exchange the kilts and bagpipes for battle dresses and light machine guns.

1. Paratroopers ; 2. Glider and airborne pilot ; 3. British Royal Marines commando ; 4. War correspondent ; 5. Special Air Service ; 6. 50th Infantry Division ; 7. 11th Armored Division ; 8. 53rd Inf. ; 9. 43rd Inf. ; 10. 59th Inf. ; 11. 15th Inf. ; 12. 7th Arm'D ; 13. British Troops in France ; 14. 49th Inf. ; 15. 79th Arm'D ; 16. 51st Inf. ; 17. 3rd Inf. ; 18. 12th Corps ; 19. Support and Service units ; 20. Scottish regiment badges (infantry) ; 21. Cavalry regiments and units ; 22. Infantry regiments ; 23. Cameronian Highlanders Glengarry ; 24. Gordon Highlanders Glengarry ; 25. Regimental cap from the East Yorkshire Regiment ; 26. Service cap for Army Territorial Service.

# of Old England

« Glengarry » caps.

20

21

22

23

24

25

26

RECONNAISSANCE

ROYAL ARMOURED CORPS

WELSH GUARDS

GRENADIER GUARDS

K.R.R.C.

ROYAL NORFOLK

MIDDLESEX

LINCOLN

QUEEN'S

DORSET

ROYAL ULSTER RIFLES

OXF. & BUCKS.

RIFLE BRIGADE

GREEN HOWARDS

EAST YORKSHIRE

SUFFOLK

SOMERSET L.I.

ROYAL WARWICKSHIRE

HAMPSHIRE

DEVON

There was a lively discussion yesterday in St. James' pub, a place much appreciated by military personnel. A Canadian from the 'La Chaudière' regiment was desperately trying to explain to a Frenchman with a red pompom that his "wife shows" French in a school in Quebec. Although they spoke the same language, the French sailor could not understand the Canadian.

Nevertheless, one does not need to be a linguist to know that "to show" means "to teach" in French Canadian.

Where world armies meet

Except some Americans who drive their cars at top speed, one sees almost only British uniforms in the streets of London. One never knows who is hiding under the khaki or the British Royal Air Force blue. The Commonwealth States alone send almost three million soldiers to support distant Europe in its struggle for freedom (Indians, New Zealanders, Australians, Canadians). You must carefully look at your neighbor's left shoulder to know whom you are dealing with. You can then read France, Czechoslovakia, Poland, Netherlands, Argentina, Brazil... Out of politeness, the English don't show their feelings, but they are irritated at the cosmopolitan turn of their capital. Every week one hears a different military band in the streets. Each country wants to celebrate its national holiday properly. On the 14th of July, General de Gaulle reviews the Free French Forces. A bugle has even been especially made for this occasion because the English one does not play the *Sidi Brahim* march decently.

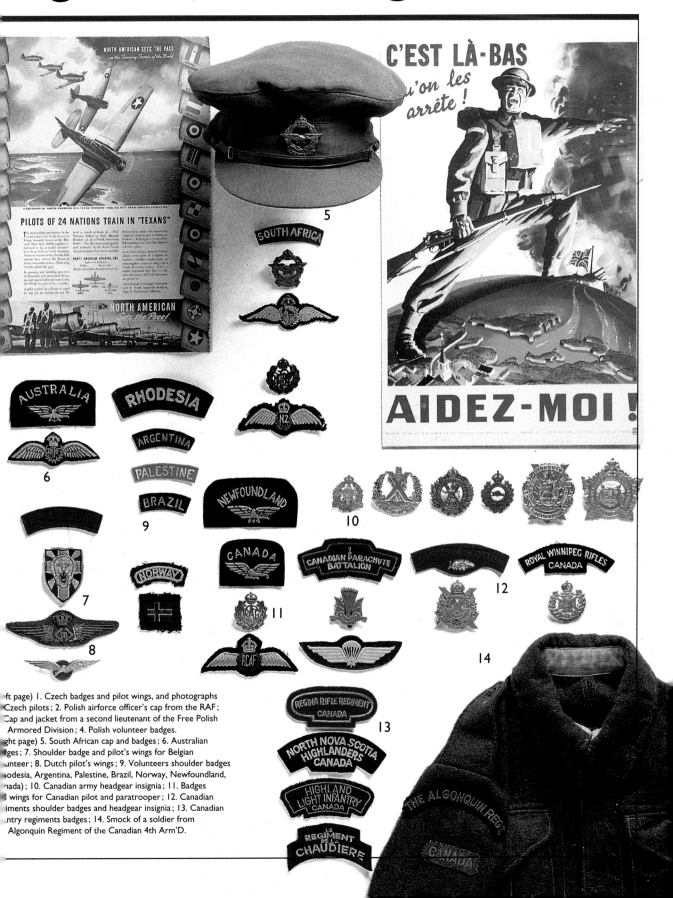

5

SOUTH AFRICA

AUSTRALIA

RHODESIA

ARGENTINA

PALESTINE

BRAZIL

6

NEWFOUNDLAND

9

CANADA

10

NORWAY

7

CANADIAN PARACHUTE BATTALION

ROYAL WINNIPEG RIFLES CANADA

12

8

11

RCAF

14

REGINA RIFLE REGIMENT CANADA

13

NORTH NOVA SCOTIA HIGHLANDERS CANADA

HIGHLAND LIGHT INFANTRY CANADA

LE REGIMENT DE LA CHAUDIÈRE

THE ALGONQUIN REG.

CANADA

(left page) 1. Czech badges and pilot wings, and photographs of Czech pilots; 2. Polish airforce officer's cap from the RAF; 3. Cap and jacket from a second lieutenant of the Free Polish 1st Armored Division; 4. Polish volunteer badges.
(right page) 5. South African cap and badges; 6. Australian badges; 7. Shoulder badge and pilot's wings for Belgian volunteer; 8. Dutch pilot's wings; 9. Volunteers shoulder badges (Rhodesia, Argentina, Palestine, Brazil, Norway, Newfoundland, Canada); 10. Canadian army headgear insignia; 11. Badges and wings for Canadian pilot and paratrooper; 12. Canadian regiments shoulder badges and headgear insignia; 13. Canadian infantry regiments badges; 14. Smock of a soldier from the Algonquin Regiment of the Canadian 4th Arm'D.

The Crown Gets

Three hundred workers have just been arbitrarily assigned to a war factory near Glasgow. Their small toy factory has been closed because it cannot be converted to make armaments. Nobody asked their opinion or took their family life into account. Workers are ordered all over the country: one day here, another there. That's a bit too much in my opinion. Where have our century-old liberties gone?

(Lower left): Collapsible stove and enameled mug, mess tin and pocket knife, ration tins, band aids and toilet kit.

Combat equipment in cotton cloth including a gas mask, a bayonet and an individual entrenching tool.

The Commonwealth: a golden mine

Although eight million British are drafted, production slows down in 1943. The British government is very quick to understand that it cannot succeed in defeating Nazi Germany alone. England contacts the Americans and members of the Commonwealth. All answers are positive. The Crown will pay the bill later. Canada builds a huge fleet on the banks of the Great Lakes. In 1944, it equals the size of the French merchant navy of 1939. South Africa participates in the battle of Africa and stops talking about leaving the Commonwealth. Australia builds 80 ships to support Great Britain, and India transforms 90 per cent of its industry into military plants.

Before the end of the war, the Crown already owes several million pounds (between 7 and 9) to its dominions and colonies.

CIGARETTES

TEA RATION 5 ozs.

BOILED SWEETS SALT & MATCHES

SHELL DRESSING

Kitted Out on Credit

...h a battle dress smock, an MKIII steel helmet with camouflage ..t, a conversation handbook and some Liberation money, ...air of spectacles and a military record book.

English Women

White shirts, black ties, cocked hats, the thirty girls in the women's navy officers' school are commanded by a female naval officer. They are listening to a male petty officer. Summoning up all his courage, he teaches them how to write official letters and concludes by saying: "To your boyfriend you can add a tear and it always works. It never works with the Admiral!" In England, 500,000 women "wear

Seventeen million "Bevin boys"

England is not America. For armaments, the English mainly depend on the United States. They are barely able to maintain their fleet at its base level, and to equip and supply existing divisions. They have good weapons, but not many of them. They have renounced improving their strategic airforce and concentrate all their efforts on the fighters. Fourteen thousand Hurricanes and 20,000 Spitfires (of which there are 47 models) control the sky. All energy is directed to this end. In 1944, 55% of the population works for the war industries.

Churchill's government includes Labour Party ministers like Attlee and Bevin and does not hesitate to take draconian measures : strikes are banned. Seventeen million English citizens, the "Bevin boys," are mobilized to increase production.

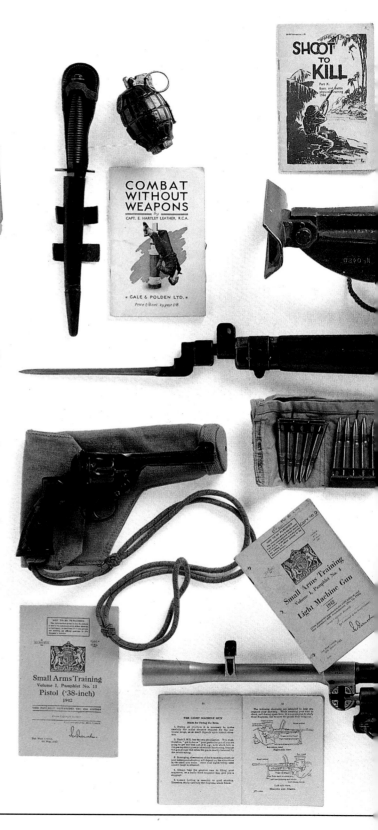

Wear the Trousers

Dagger for commandos and paratroopers; Mills n°36 grenade; Sten machine pistol MKII, 9mm caliber; 2-inch infantry mortar; Lee-Enfield n°4 rifle, 303 caliber with bayonet and canvas bandoleer with 5-cartridge clips; Enfield n°2 revolver, 38 caliber; Bren MK3 light machine gun, 303 caliber with clip.

A Duel Ove

Made contact with the American B17s over the French coast. They'd been waiting for ten minutes. For once they arrived early. Unfortunately, the German radars spotted them. A horde of FWs and MEs were there too. They encircled our formation, which spat fire in all directions. God! Every German fighter plane was there. We were out-numbered: ten to one.

The last set

After the battle of 1940-1941, the Germans realize that there is not much that they can do against England's solid defense. With this in mind, the Luftwaffe begins attacking the Allied formations which target the bunkers of the Atlantic Wall, German towns and the Ruhr. German fighters based in Saint-Omer, Abbeville, Bethune and Lille learn to expect the American B17s or B24s, and the English Halifaxes and Lancasters when the Allied planes leave England or when they return from their mission. It is a matter of minutes and the timing must be perfect. The British Squadron fighters work to protect bombers and bring them back intact. If they arrive too late or too soon, the result is catastrophic. German fighters take off and harass Allied planes. It is under these circumstances that René Mouchotte, a French pilot of the FAFL (*Force française aérienne libre*, the Free French Air Force), commanding the "Alsace" group, dies on the 27th of August 1943. His plane crashes into the sea. On the same day, five Allied planes are shot down and seven German aircraft fail to return to their base.

Left to right, top to bottom : flight book ; military record, certificate, photo and medals of an air gunner from a Lancaster bomber ; pilot goggles, flight helmet and oxygen mask ; Airforce officer's jacket and cap, decorated with the Distinguished Flying Cross, a medal awarded for bravery ; silk escape maps and survival ration ; Irvin sheepskin flight jacket and Mae West life jacket ; RAF flight handbooks and booklets ; cigarette box.

Sten, Quee

Enfin des renseignements sur les armes parachutées. On ne sait pas toujours comment ça marche. Au fond du container «Le manuel du saboteur»:

La Sten est une arme très efficace pour le combat de près... Elle ne saurait être substituée au fusil de guerre... On recommande le coup par coup car ar le tir est plus juste et économique —

Ça on s'en est aperçu!

French Army revolver (1892 model) with leather case; US revolver Smith & Wess 38 caliber; American automatic pistol, C 1911 AI, 45 caliber; British magnetic mi Clam MKIII; British grenade, Mills n°36 British grenade, Gammon; German stick grenade.

At last there is information about the parachuted weapons. We're not always certain how they work. At the bottom of the container: The Saboteur Textbook. "The Sten is a very efficient weapon for close combat. However it cannot replace the war rifle. We recommend shooting single rounds because firing is more precise and economic." We had already realized that!

A star: the Colt

Over 418,083 weapons are parachuted to the French Resistance: 196,500 submachine guns, mostly Stens, 57,849 pistols and revolvers, 20,904 light machine guns, 8,361 USM1 rifles and 4,180 anti-tank weapons. The English submachine gun plays a very important role. It becomes the symbol of the *Maquis*. An awkward-looking weapon, it is difficult to take seriously. It is a mass of quickly assembled pieces of sheet metal and has the unfortunate reputation of opening fire at the smallest knock. An exceptional weapon, cheap and quickly made, it has its unconditional fans and adamant enemies. Four models are produced. The last one at the end of 1943 is a real submachine gun. The Colts are second in fame only to the Stens. The Allies can't keep up with a great demand. Anti-tank weapons are only delivered to the French Resistance in 1944.

of the Maquis

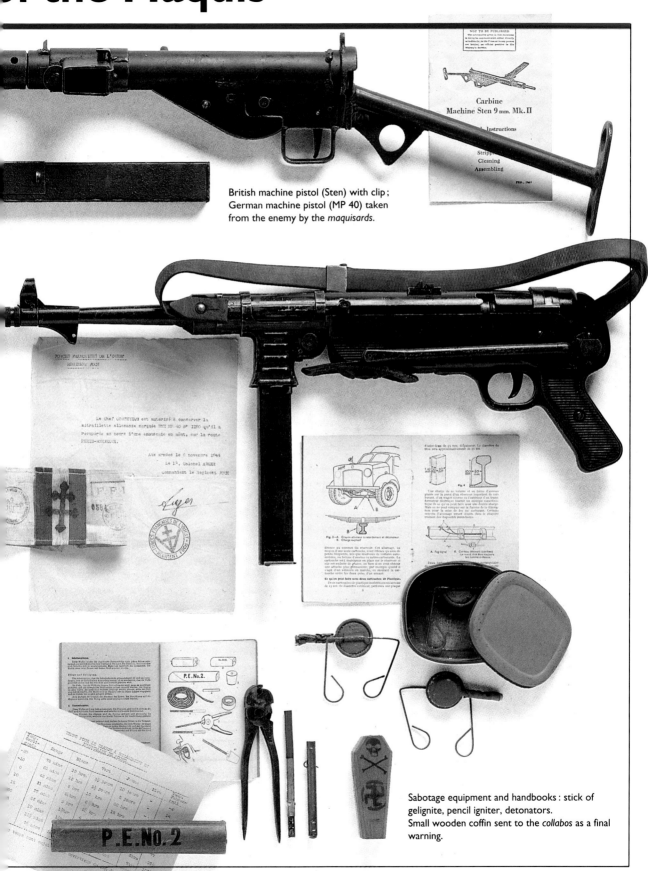

British machine pistol (Sten) with clip ; German machine pistol (MP 40) taken from the enemy by the *maquisards*.

Sabotage equipment and handbooks : stick of gelignite, pencil igniter, detonators.
Small wooden coffin sent to the *collabos* as a final warning.

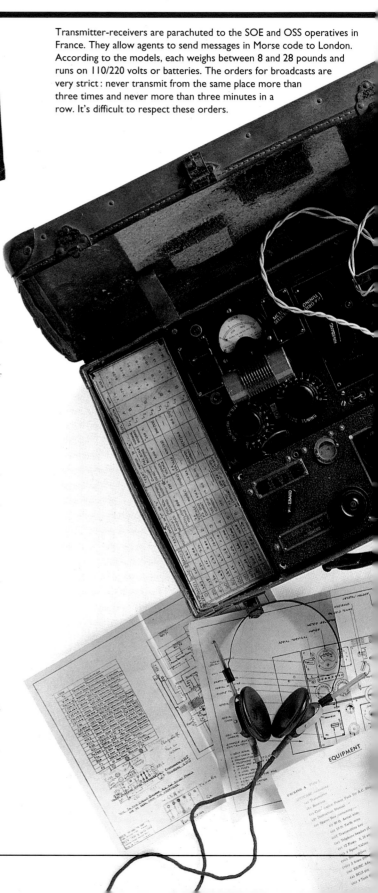

Chargé de la protection d'une équipe parachutée de Londres.

Le PIANISTE est repéré alors qu'il transmet. Coupure de courant dans l'immeuble. Heureusement il continue à émettre avec la batterie de la traction que j'ai monté dans la chambre.

Les Allemands en civil sont là. Ils n'y voient que du feu. Ils coupent le courant ailleurs pour savoir si ça émet toujours.

Doigt sur la détente, derrière la porte. Je ne bouge pas. Quelle sacrée trouille!

I was in charge of the protection of a team parachuted from London. The "pianist" was spotted during a transmission. Power to the building was cut. Luckily he was able to continue transmitting with the car battery that I took up to his room. The Germans plain clothes men were completely taken in. They cut electricity to another building to check if the transmission stopped. With my finger on the trigger, I waited behind the door without making a move, scared to death.

Transmitter-receivers are parachuted to the SOE and OSS operatives in France. They allow agents to send messages in Morse code to London. According to the models, each weighs between 8 and 28 pounds and runs on 110/220 volts or batteries. The orders for broadcasts are very strict: never transmit from the same place more than three times and never more than three minutes in a row. It's difficult to respect these orders.

Set Europe ablaze

To keep abreast of German troop movements, the Allies parachute in agents, or send them by boat or plane. The agents must transmit the information collected by the Resistance intelligence networks back to London and then organize sabotage missions. The radio operator, the "pianist", plays the principal role. He transmits messages in Morse code during his daily broadcasts, and then listens for the answers on "Personal messages." The "pianist" is targeted in this ruthless war. His life expectancy is three months. When caught, the Germans torture him and try to force him to transmit false information. If he refuses, he is shot immediately. All the secret Allied services send spies: the Intelligence Secret Services, the mysterious Special Operations Executive, the Office of Strategic Service, the BCRA. When they are not actively fighting each other, they often ignore each other. Churchill has given them only one order: "Set Europe ablaze".

he Pianist

The functioning of this decoding machine is rather simple, and, therefore, not very reliable, especially when the enemy succeeds in seizing one. This happens several times during the war. The Germans often understand the messages sent by the Allies and vice versa.

Trois heures qu'on attend dans les fourrés au bord du terrain. On se sert de feux de bois comme balises. Trois au centre du terrain à 100 mètres de distance. A droite une torche pour les signaux optiques. Le lieutenant fait signe. Il vient d'entendre l'appareil dans son S PHONE. Un Halifax. On bondit. J'allume les feux. L'avion passe. 3 fois. Les containers sont au bout du champ. Opération terminée. On remballe et on calte -

We waited for three hours in the bushes along the parachuting field. We made beacons out of firewood. Three in the center of the field, 100 yards from each other. On the right we had a flashlight for light signals. The lieutenant made a sign when he heard the plane over his S Phone. A Halifax. We jumped to our feet and I lit the fires. The plane made three passes before the containers fell at the edge of the field. Then the operation was over. We packed up and took off.

Meetings on moonless nights

From 1941 to 1944, the British parachute weapons and military equipment to France. In the beginning, "parcels" are designated for Resistance fighters. Later they go to the Jedburgh teams: 3 men – one French, one American and one British – behind the lines. Eighty-six Jedburgh teams maneuver in France to sabotage strategic targets.

Parachuting operations are carefully prepared. A chosen field must be approved by London and "orders" must be put through. Using "Personal messages", the BBC reports the acceptance of a field and communicates which moonless night the operation is authorized to occur.

For the Resistants, the worst is still to come. Beacons must be placed on the Dropping Zone – the parachuting field –, planes must be guided, "goods" need to be collected, parachutes buried, weapons collected and hidden in a safe place, and containers need to be destroyed.

Opening the parachuted containers, the Resistance fighters discover weapons sent by the British government: Mills grenades, Bren light machine gun, Sten machine pistol, Lee-Enfield rifle.

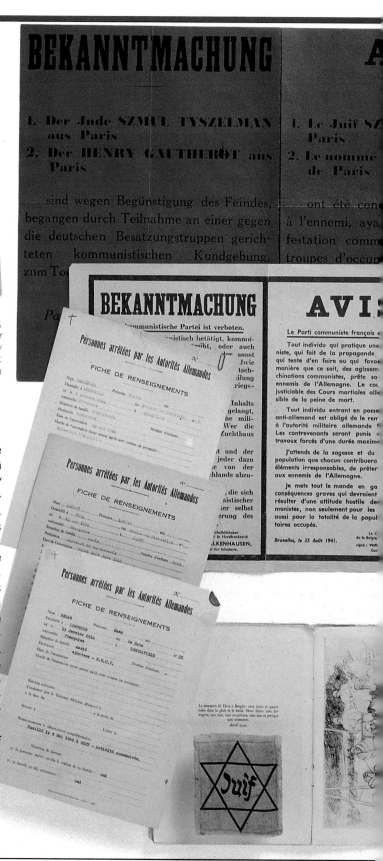

Ce matin, en croisant Mme Klein (sans nouvelles de son mari depuis 10 jours), j'ai pensé à Hélène, mon amie d'enfance. Elle aussi avait dû coudre une étoile jaune sur son manteau. Voilà un an que je ne l'ai pas revue...

Des bruits circulent; les Juifs sont emmenés en Allemagne dans des camps de travail. Mais que se passe-t-il au juste?

I thought about my childhood girlfriend Helena this morning, when I met Mrs. Klein, who has had no news from her husband for ten days. She was also forced to sew a yellow star on her coat. It's already been a year since I've seen her. Rumor has it that Jews are taken to work camps in Germany. What happens to them?

Hostages don't even do the trick

Two hundred and fifty thousand people deported. 76,000 Jews (22,000 of them French) are sent to the death camps. Only 2,500 will come back! Some 30,000 Resistance fighters and hostages are executed. No one knows the exact number of victims who fall to Nazism in France.

Hostages are taken among the people arrested by the Germans or the French. Each *Kommandantur* has a list of 150 names of hostages (in Paris the number is between 300 and 400). Occupying forces choose their victims in the following order: politicians, government officials, intellectuals, "dangerous persons." The Resistance is so sure of its eventual victory that it takes no heed of General de Gaulle's request that no unnecessary bomb attacks or murder attempts be made, in order to spare the population. Even the almighty Oberg, chief of the German police, admits that the "present situation could not be improved with punishments or collective measures."

Poster

ORDONNANCE
concernant les actes de sabotage et de pillage

Abs. 1

Wer es unternimmt, Sabotage an Einrichtungen oder Eigentum der deutschen Wehrmacht oder ihrer Angehörigen - z. B. an Waffen aller Art, Beutestücken, Vorräten, Magazinen, Kabel- oder sonstigen Nachrichtenleitungen - zu verüben oder die Wirtschaft im besetzten Gebiet zu sabotieren, wird mit dem Tode bestraft. In leichteren Fällen, kann Zuchthaus auf Zeit oder Lebenszeit verhängt werden.

Abs. 2

Die gleiche Strafe trifft denjenigen, welcher es unternimmt :
a) Die allgemeinen Verkehrsmittel wie Wege, Brücken, Eisenbahnen, usw... zu beschädigen.
b) Zu plündern ;
c) Eigentumsvergehen aller Art an den im Abschnitt I genannten Einrichtungen oder Gegenständen zu verüben.

Die Gemeinden

Par. 1

Quiconque commettra des actes de sabotage à des installations ou à la propriété de l'autorité militaire allemande ou de ses membres propres, à des armes de tout genre, des butins, des stocks, des dépôts, des câbles ou d'autres moyens de communication ou quiconque sabotera l'économie dans la région occupée sera frappé de peine de mort.

Dans des cas moins graves une peine de travaux forcés temporaire ou à perpétuité sera imposée.

Par. 2

Des mêmes peines sera frappé celui :
a) Qui endommagera les moyens de transports, tels que routes, ponts, chemins de fer, etc...;
b) Qui pillera ;
c) Qui commettra des contraventions de toutes sortes aux installations et objets cités dans le Par. I.

Par. 3

La commune de la scène du crime ainsi que celle de la résidence du coupable, répondront par leurs habitants aux dommages causés par les actes cités dans les Par. I et 2.

Par. 4

Cette ordonnance est valable pour les départements du Pas-de-Calais et du Nord et entrera en vigueur le jour de sa publication. 'Lille, le 21 Juin 1940.

Le Commandant de l'Oberfeldkommandantur 670,

Those who lived under Nazi rule will always remember it as a reign of humiliation and terror.

The newsagent gave me a tip. She said that the addresses for good, well-supplied and well-heated places are in the Pariser Zeitung. She was right. On page 5, there is a map with the cafés, restaurants and shops where one can forget about the war and one's hunger. You don't have to speak German to understand. In these places tickets aren't necessary, just banknotes.

An unreceived signal

The German press in France immediately lays its cards on the table: it's the victor's press. Mostly published in German, there is an occasional French edition. This is true in the case of *Signal* and the *Pariser Zeitung*. German newspapers don't have many readers.

Dr Goebbels, the leader of the *Propaganda Staffel* and a shrewd man, is fascinated by communication. He admires Churchill who promises "blood, toil, tears and sweat", unlike the French who trumpet "we shall win because we are the best". Having graduated from Heidelberg University with a doctorate in literature, he prefers Mozart to Wagner. Despite his good-natured looks, he is a fearsome hard-liner and leads his fellow countrymen to total war.

Propaganda

Coup fumant!
Georges a les plans du MUR du
Havre à Cherbourg.
STRENG GEHEIM : ultra secret
Réussit à se faire embaucher
comme peintre chez Todt.
Les plans sont sur la table.
Il les sort dans un rouleau
de papier peint destiné
à tapisser le bureau
du Bauleiter.
Et un aller simple
pour Londres!

A master stroke! Georges has the plans to the "Wall" from Le Havre to Cherbourg. Strenggeheim: top secret. He managed to get hired as a painter for the Todt Organization. The plans were on the table, and he got them out in a roll of wallpaper for the Bauleiter's office. And they went straight to London!

The biggest fortress of all time

To build the "Atlantic Wall", 13.3 million tons of concrete are poured on the beaches of France by the Todt Organization. The Wall is supposed to prevent any Allied landing. To build the site, the Todt Organization, the Engineers Corps of the German Army, hires 260,000 French workers in 1942. These well-paid volunteers are then replaced by labor conscripts from the STO. The 9,300 outworks of the wall are distributed along 1,250 miles from Holland to Biarritz. They are defended by 10,000 mines. In 1943, Marshal Rommel reinforces the anti-aircraft batteries with guns (from the 75-caliber to the 406-caliber gun) and sets up obstacles designed to hamper a possible landing: "Rommel's asparagus," "lion's teeth." The fortress is reputed to be unassailable. In spite of these gigantic efforts, the Wall is not finished and it contains many faults which Resistance agents inform London about. The Allies breach it on the 6th of June 1944.

Concrete on the Beaches

Todt Organization arm band.

Anti-aircraft (flak) shell, 20 mm caliber.

Shell head with Navy artillery container 77 mm caliber.

On the *Reichkriegsflagge* (1), left to right and top to bottom : fake mine (lure) in concrete ; camouflaged helmet of Navy artillery, « Tellermine » anti-tank mine with transport box ; antipersonnel concrete mine ; antipersonnel glass mine ; reproduction of a gun from the Lindeman battery in Pas-de-Calais.

(1) War flag from the Third Reich, model of the Kriegsmarine (Navy).

*Assisté de loin au bombar-
-dement du bunker de
WIZERNES–
Objectif signalé à Londres il
y a 3 mois. Une base de
lancement de V2.
Capacité 100 fusées par jour!
Les Anglais ont mis le paquet.
Enormes explosions.
Mais le béton est tellement
épais ...
Un avion abattu, trois para-
-chutes ne se sont pas
ouverts. Ils ont sauté
trop tard!*

*I watched the bombing of Wizernes bunker from far away, a
target reported to London three months ago. It's a site which
can launch 100 V2s per day! The English spared no bombs.
There were huge explosions, but the concrete is so thick!
One plane was shot down. Three parachutes didn't work.
The pilots jumped too late.*

A well stocked arsenal

Until the end of WW2 the Third Reich
maintains an astonishing capacity for
producing military equipment. In 1944, the
Germans manufacture 36,000 planes (13,000
more than England and nearly as many as
the USSR). The Focke Wulff 190, a very
quick fighter, replaces the Stukas, to the
great displeasure of the Royal Air Force.
Equipped with 2 to 4 guns and machine
guns, 20,000 planes of this type are
produced.

During the war, the Germans produce twice
as many tanks as the British, in spite of 5.5
million drafted men. There are also the
secret weapons: V1, V2, V3. Nine thousand
V2s are launched on England and 6,000 on
Antwerp even as the Germans are moving
out. German tanks (Tigers, Koenigsters,
Panthers) outclass those of the Allies. The
Messerschmitt 262 jet fighter is operational
but can't be mass produced efficiently
enough to reverse the course of the war.
The A-Bomb cannot be completed by the
Germans before 1947, at best.

Hitler's Last Hope

...sault rifle (Sturmgewehr), MP44, 7.92 caliber Kurtz;
...8 pistol, 9mm caliber and P08 pistol, 9mm caliber; stick
...nade; MG42 machine gun, 7.92mm caliber and drum
...gazine with 50-shot belt; MP40 Schmeisser machine
...tol, 9mm caliber; 98K Mauser rifle, 7.92 mm caliber with
...k and 5-cartridge clips; 98K Mauser bayonet with steel
...ath.

Shok troups have found a way to improve their pay. They sell their prisonners to guys in the rear who are only too happy to play the hero and brag about prisonners they've supposedly taken.

Each rank has its price. They even dressed a "Feldwebel" as a general in order to get more dollars!..

Collar patches : 1. Army General; 2. Army Officer; 3. Airforce Officer; 14. Army soldiers.

Unrest amongst the German Generals

Very quickly after the lost battle of Stalingrad in 1943, many high-ranking officers criticize Hitler's actions. The revolt peaks as the Führer decides to take the direction of military operations in hand. Plots are organized to kill him.

A murder attempt fails on the 20th of July 1944, resulting in the deportation of thousands of opponents or execution and the demotion of officers. Marshal Rommel is obliged to commit suicide.

Ten months before the end of the war, the Führer counts on the V1s and V2s to win but their launching pads are destroyed by the Allies. There are no longer enough jet planes in production.

On several occasions rebellious generals contact the Allies who neither help nor encourage them.

10. Stabsfeldwebel (Warrant Officer class I); 11. Oberfeldwebel (W.O. class 2); 12. Oberfähnrich (Officer Cadet); 13. Feldwebel (Sergeant); 15. Unterfeldwebel (Sergeant); 16. Unteroffizier (Corporal); 17. Soldier and lance corporal.

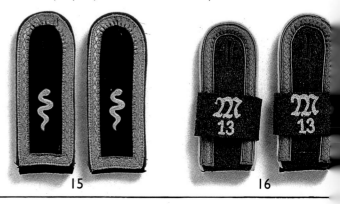

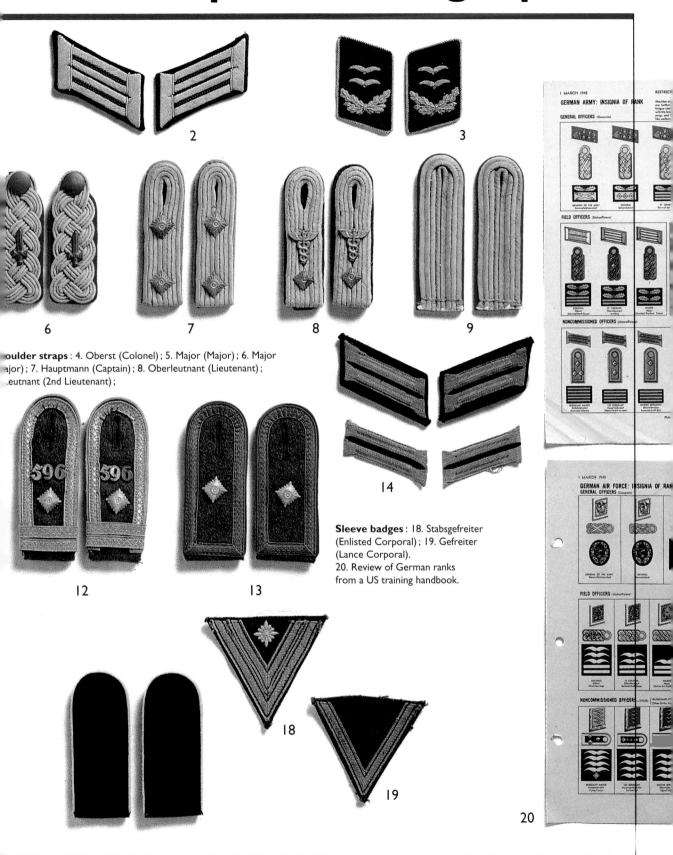

Shoulder straps : 4. Oberst (Colonel) ; 5. Major (Major) ; 6. Major (Major) ; 7. Hauptmann (Captain) ; 8. Oberleutnant (Lieutenant) ; Leutnant (2nd Lieutenant) ;

Sleeve badges : 18. Stabsgefreiter (Enlisted Corporal) ; 19. Gefreiter (Lance Corporal).
20. Review of German ranks from a US training handbook.

Today, we identified an SS badge on a prisoner's uniform.

According to our intelligence officer, this guy belongs to the "Leibstandarte" Adolf Hitler division.

The regiments of body guards, reorganized a few weeks ago, come from the Russian front. Their weapons are excellent. They even have Tiger Tanks.

Luftwaffe breast eagle
(German airforce).

Iron Cross 1st class
1939.

Belt buckle
for a Luftwaffe trooper.

Eagles and swastikas are omnipresent on German badges. The eagle has appeared on the military uniforms of many countries because it symbolizes power. As for the swastika, emblem of the Nazi Party, it is an obscure symbol of occult relations with evil spirits.

Hitler's Praetorian Guard goes to the fire

If Hitler still controls his moribund country with an iron hand in 1944, he owes it to the SS. The *Schutzstaffel* were originally designed to protect the Führer. These fanatics currently reign over Germany.

When Himmler developed the SS after Hitler took power, he created a parallel hierarchy which quickly seized control of the State and Party. The SS come to supervise everything from economy to propaganda and... the Army. They intervene whenever they want.

The SS are themselves an army within the army: there are 4 divisions in 1940, 36 in 1944. SS soldiers are dressed in camouflage uniforms and their badge represents a death's head. It is from the hard core of the SS that the Waffen SS are organized. In 1944, several divisions, including Hitler's praetorian guard, fight in Normandy.

Candidates for the SS are recruited among the Hitlerian Youths. They are first given an intense political training and then, when they pass all the necessary tests, they swear to obey the Führer till their death and receive the dagger of honor.

Combat badges

Airborne infantry
Luftwaffe

Flak
(anti-aircraft)
Luftwaffe

Panzertruppe
(tanks)

Trapezoidal field cap badge (1943 model)
for a Wehrmacht Heer trooper.

Navy destroyers
(Kriegsmarine)

On Our Side!

Wehrmacht Heer breast eagle
(Army).

Iron Cross 2nd class,
1939.

Trapezoidal cap badge (1943 model)
for a Waffen SS trooper.

Belt buckle
for a Wehrmacht Heer trooper.

Close combat badge.

Belt buckle
for a Waffen SS trooper.

Sport badge.

Assault badge,
all corps.

Assault badge,
infantry.

Badge for wounded
soldiers, bronze model.

Commemorative arm badges for battles on the Eastern front
(Kuban, Crimea and Demiansk); review of German medals from a US Army
training handbook.

On my way to Ireland, on one of these famous Liberty Ships, mass. produced in Frisco.

They're not sturdy. They break in two when the weather gets too rough.

For quicker assembly, prefabricated elements are welded instead of riveted.

For my boys, it's a joke — either it works or it sinks —

A fistful of dollars

To forge – from start to finish – the first world army inside three years, that is the American challenge in 1941. All factories are mobilized to participate in the war effort. Ten million more wage-earners are hired in four years. Fifteen million women are employed as crane operators, welders and heavy plant drivers. Car manufacturers assemble planes, and washing machine manufacturers fix turrets for machine guns. They proclaim their patriotism, prize it greatly and advertize it. It works!

Americans tighten their belts.

There is not a new car for sale in the whole country. But, on the West Coast, a "liberty ship" is assembled in 15 days. This does not happen without complications. The flux of manpower toward the factories provokes many problems including housing shortages. Roosevelt is obliged to make a special decree enabling Black Americans to work in plants and forbidding any discrimination.

Make Machine-Guns Now

Josette est tombée follement amoureuse d'un soldat américain: Patrick. Il est grand, mince, beau. Et en plus il vient du Texas!

Elle a cousu sur sa blouse un gros insigne U.S. Deux galons avec un T au milieu.

Impossible de savoir ce qu'il fait là-bas, ni pour combien de temps il est ici.

Nous nous sommes toutes les deux mis à l'anglais avec "Assimil."

Josette, my girlhood friend, has fallen madly in love with an American soldier named Patrick. He's tall, slim and handsome. And to top it all he's from Texas! She sewed a big US badge on her blouse. Two stripes with a T in the middle. Impossible to know what he does here or how long he'll stay here. We've both started learning English with the Assimil method.

My beloved cowboy!

"When are we getting married, my beloved cowboy?" Everyone sings to this tune launched by the radio.

For many French women, Prince Charming is dressed in khaki this summer. They fight over the American boys. Every night, beautiful soldiers sporting impeccably pleated trousers dance in the squares to the music of an accordion with young women dressed in large corolla skirts. Stripes from the left sleeves of GIs now adorn the breasts of French girls. The ranks of the American Army hold no secrets from them. Sometimes they mistake their new Gods. They might take the blacksmith from a farm in Colorado for a rich landowner. Never mind: he is American.

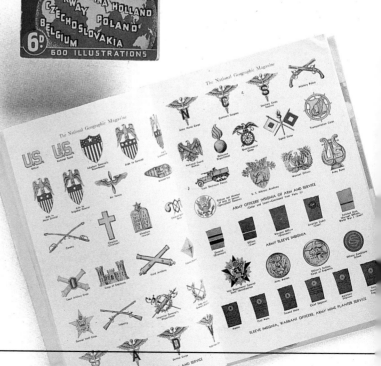

1. Non-commissioned and enlisted men's cap badge; 2. Officer's cap badge; 3. Warrant Officer; 4. 2nd Lieutenant; 5. 1st Lieutenant; 6. Captain; 7. Major; 8. Lieutenant-Colonel; 9. Colonel; 10. Overseas Service chevrons; 11. 3rd grade Technician; 12. Staff-Sergeant; 13. Technical Sergeant; 14. 1st Sergeant; 15. Master Sergeant; 16. Private 1st class; 17. 5th grade Technician; 18. Corporal; 19. 4th grade Technician; 20. Sergeant.

« Ike » jacket and flight officer's cap, glider pilot from the US Army Air Force, 1945.

Superbes ces insignes américains. J'ai fait monter deux écussons US en boucles d'oreilles. C'est un peu gros mais original. En broche, j'ai un insigne et aviateur. Au bout d'une chaine, l'emblème du "Signal corps". Les insignes brillent sous le soleil comme de l'or. Et je ne fais que commencer ma collection!

SHAEF (Supreme Headquarter Allied Expeditionary Forces).
Airborne Troop Carrier H.Q., 1st Army, 3rd Army, 1st Allied Airborne.

Armored Divisions and Tank Destroyers.

17th, 82nd and 101st Airborne divisions.

Cap badges for Paratroopers and Gliders.

These American badges are good stuff. I had two of them made into earrings. They are a little big, but very original. At the end of a chain hangs the emblem of the Signal Corps. The gold on the badges shines in the sun. And I'm only at the start of my collection!

The American miracle

Strongly impressed by the uniforms, badges and presence of the Wehrmacht soldiers four years before, Frenchmen – and especially Frenchwomen – are ecstatic when they see the American soldiers' battle-dresses with multiple pockets.

The badges – whether they are in relief on a copper background for soldiers or delicately cut for officers – shine like gold. They adorn the shirts of the women who chase souvenirs. This new army, which sweeps through France in long convoys, is not made of severe and brutal supermen. These are real men with nice smiles; they are prepared to die when necessary, but also seem to believe that they will never have to. The army itself is not exactly an army anymore. Its PX – supply warehouses – and its Supply Corps make it look sometimes like an advertisement caravan parading to *In the Mood*, Glenn Miller's hit.

the Gold Rush

1st · 2nd · 3rd · 4th · 5th · 8th

10th · 26th · 28th · 29th · 30th

MOUNTAIN

35th · 36th · 42nd · 44th · 45th

63rd · 65th · 66th · 69th · 70th · 71st

76th · 78th · 79th · 80th · 83rd

85th · 86th · 87th · 88th · 89th

91st · 92nd · 94th · 95th · 96th

100th · 102nd · 103rd · 104th · 106th

Peace is America's
Most Important Business!

You can be proud of your new Army . . .
An Army of Specialists—strong, resourceful—
advancing science, fitting men for new and satisfying careers.
An Army of Opportunity . . . where leadership, initiative,
ability are required, recognized, rewarded.
An Army with One Great Purpose . . . PEACE!

There is opportunity for every young man in the new U. S. Army. You can get full details at any U. S. Army and U. S. Air Force Recruiting Station.

AIRBORNE
MOUNTAIN
AIRBORNE

The U. S. Army—Part Of The Team—For Security
Army Day-April 6

Know your new Army better. Visit your nearest Army post, camp or station.

Infantry Divisions (North-West Europe and Italy
campaigns).
Above : M1 Liner helmet with lance corporal
badges from the « Go Devils » 60th Infantry
Regiment of the 9th Infantry Division.
Lower left : Special Forces paratrooper badge,
Rangers Battalion badge, and jacket of a technical
sergeant from the 29th Infantry Division ;
infantryman collar badge ; breast badge (Combat
Infantryman badge) and ribbons (Army Good
Conduct, European Theatre of Operations and
Victory Medal)

C'est bath d'être habillée à l'américaine! D'habitude, je taille dans mes vieilles jupes pour rapiécer tant bien que mal un manteau. Mais cette année, je peux me confectionner un nouveau manteau dans une couverture kaki US toute neuve. Une amie a trouvé une couverture de la RAF bleu pétrole. Pas mal non plus!

For GIs : a wool cap, some canvas field equipment, combat field jacket, K-rations, toiletry kit, laced boots with rubber soles and a rubber raincoat.

It's really super to dress American style. Usually I cut into my old skirts to patch up my coat as well as I can. This year I made a new coat out of a brand new American khaki blanket instead. A friend of mine found an airforce blue blanket from the RAF. Not bad either!

Ice cream and Coca Cola go to the front line

All American soldiers' material means are put at disposal so that they can keep up their strength, energy and morale. Everything has been studied so that they won't lack anything, from condoms to pocket books, not to mention Coke.

Their battle dresses are as efficient as they are varied. From the double helmet, heavy and light, to the tireless rangers. Relief no longer has to edge its way through tight trenches, like during WWI. The soldiers are not obliged to wait for the field kitchen anymore.

GIs, and tank destroyers with their bazookas too, go to the front line in armored halftracks. Their vehicles are armed with half-inch machine guns and carry the soldiers' individual rations for 24 hours. Supplies and munitions follow.

Shermans Attack

Present Arms!

For the five million Americans who cross the Atlantic to fight in Europe, nothing is too good. The American government has allowed for all sorts of vehicles to transport its troops flawlessly and has also made sure that the troops lack nothing. Individual equipment is functional and designed for each season and each country. Weapons are particularly efficient.

The M1 rifle made by Winchester, for example, is a specially well-conceived weapon. Semi-automatic, it only weighs 5 pounds, is 3 feet long and has an effective range of approximately 3,000 yards. Its clip contains 15 thirty-caliber cartridges. It is coveted by all (the French Resistance received only a small quantity — less than 10,000).

With 100,000 tanks, 2.3 million trucks, 61,000 guns and a Signals Corps nearly as efficient as those of the Germans, the American army is devastatingly powerful. Both its size and the conditions under which it directs combat are awesome.

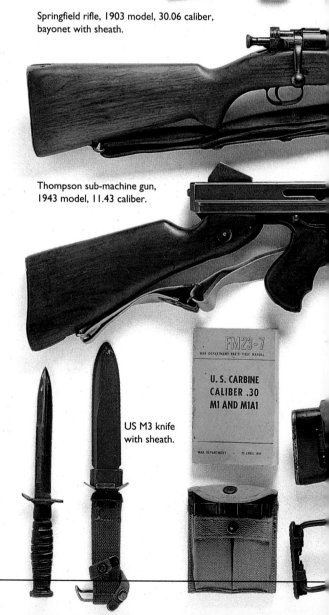

Semi-automatic rifle, Garand M1, 30.06 caliber, 8-cartrige metal clips with canvas bandoleer clip carrier, bayonet with sheath.

Springfield rifle, 1903 model, 30.06 caliber, bayonet with sheath.

Thompson sub-machine gun, 1943 model, 11.43 caliber.

US M3 knife with sheath.

FM23-7
WAR DEPARTMENT BASIC FIELD MANUAL

U. S. CARBINE CALIBER .30 M1 AND M1A1

WAR DEPARTMENT · 23 APRIL 1944

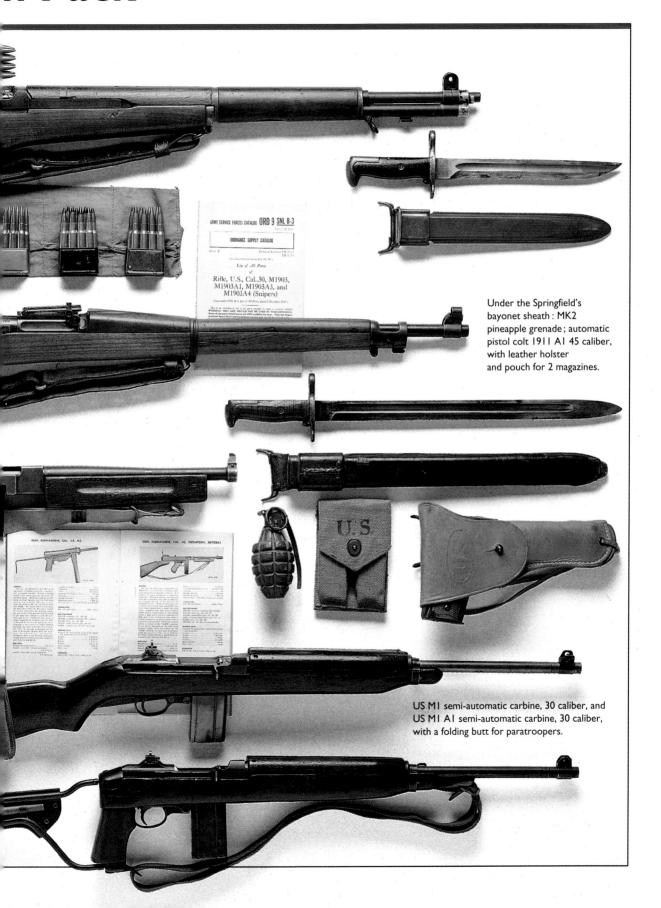

ARMY SERVICE FORCES CATALOG **ORD 9 SNL B-3**

List of All Parts

ORDNANCE SUPPLY CATALOG

Group B

Technical Reference FM 23-10
TM 1-215

(Standard Nomenclature List No. B-3)

List of All Parts

of

Rifle, U.S., Cal..30, M1903,
M1903A1, M1903A3, and
M1903A4 (Snipers)

(Supersedes SNL B-3, List of All Parts, dated 2 December 1943.)

Under the Springfield's
bayonet sheath : MK2
pineapple grenade ; automatic
pistol colt 1911 A1 45 caliber,
with leather holster
and pouch for 2 magazines.

US M1 semi-automatic carbine, 30 caliber, and
US M1 A1 semi-automatic carbine, 30 caliber,
with a folding butt for paratroopers.

Just back from a Suffolk flying fortress base. It's pure America at home! A tall M.P, armed with a Colt by his side, regulates traffic on the base. Thirty feet away, one of our policemen, in white gloves, does the same for the small village. They ignore each other. The Jeeps tear past. Their uniforms are a disgrace; they make all the soldiers look like mechanics.

The fortresses unroll their carpet of bombs

Carefully camouflaged, the American "flying fortresses" wait at the base for their departure signal. At the American barracks in England, one can live American style. The crew's eccentric uniforms, especially their headgear, make His Majesty's officers chill. On base one moves around only by car. It's in a Jeep that nine crew members go to their "ship" to take off after watching a film of their flight, checking the meteorological conditions and reviewing numerous photos taken by reconnaissance planes in order to spot the target exactly. With their sheepskin lined leather jackets, oxygen masks, loads of photos and maps and all their equipment, they look like big awkward bears.

Protected by 13 machine guns, the huge planes take off one by one. They circle around the base in order to leave in formation and move in the direction of Germany to unroll their carpet of bombs.

Left to right, top to bottom: pilot cap; Airforce officer cap; photo-albums from a P38 Lightning pilot; wooden bomb decorated with drawings; survival rations and postcards; aviator's wings; goggles, flight helmet and oxygen mask; 8th and 9th US Army Air Force badges; Ray-Ban sunglasses; flight watch; luminous pen; military record and identification plate; flashlight; flight glove; flight boot; flight map bag; A2 jacket.

Spreads its Wings

The Dakota is absolutely extraordinary! On D-day several squadrons dropped paratroopers and equipment over France. One of the planes was hit by a falling container. Consequence: six feet of its right wing broken off and an engine out of action. The Dakota turned back and calmly landed on its English airfield.

The Willys Jeep, a small four-wheel drive vehicle used for reconnaissance missions.

A four-wheel Dodge ambulance; toy made by an American soldier wounded during the Italy campaign.

A little car unlike all others

Jeep, GMC, Sherman. Three names which sound triumphantly in the ears of the liberated populations. The Jeep is a general purpose vehicle used in reconnaissance operations, and even in attacks, when equipped with machine guns. Five hundred thousand Jeeps are produced. Even the Jeep's most enthusiastic fans, however, claim it provokes more deaths than the war because of its instability. Nicknamed the "beast of burden", GMC has 3 bearing axles, a range of 210 miles (plus jerricans). One million GMCs are built and 100,000 are delivered to the USSR.

More than 50,000 Shermans are produced. Thanks to their mobility and tireless engine, they win the battle of the tanks. The Dakota, the first plane entirely made out of iron, was mass produced: one million aircraft are made during WW2. All the American motors use the same spare parts. They are followed by travelling workshops which fix and repair vehicles as quickly as possible.

Tens of thousands of big Studebaker Trucks move the men and supplies of war

a Skybus

Plastic model of the Hawker Hurricane fighter plane.

e C47 Dakota, used by the
es to transport troops and
ipment.

uction models
e German « Tiger »
pfwVI tank, and of
USM4A3 « Sherman »

5 juin 44

Cette fois ça y est!
Ils débarquent! On vient de l'entendre dans les messages personnels de Londres:
LES SANGLOTS LONGS DES VIOLONS DE L'AUTOMNE.
et LA LUNE EST PLEINE D'ÉLÉPHANTS VERTS —

Le capitaine le dit : ce sont les phrases code. Kaput les Fridolins. On sort les Stens mises au frais dans les containers.

Depuis le temps qu'on attend ça!

This is it. They're landing. We just heard it from London over personal messages: "The long sobs of the autumn violins." And "The moon is full of green elephants." The captain says: "These are the key coded sentences. Kaput the Jerries. Time to take the Stens out of their containers. We have been waiting for this moment for so long."

Radio Paris lies, Radio Paris is German

With drawn curtains and hidden lights, thousands of French people listen to the English radio every night, at their own risk. At 9:15 P.M., the first notes of Beethoven's *Fifth Symphony* (the V for Victory translated into Morse code notes: ti-ti-ti-ta), give their four knocks. "Here is London. Today is the 456th day of the struggle of the French population for its liberation." And on the tune of *La Cucaracha*, the speaker hums: "Radio Paris lies, Radio Paris lies, Radio Paris is German." A slogan invented by Jean Oberlé. Despite German jamming, nobody would miss this nightly appointment for anything in the world. "Personal messages" for the members of the French Resistance alternate with reports on military operations, Pierre Dac's chronicles and Jean Marin's comments. When "The French talk to to the French", people come to realize the Resistance fighter within themselves.

Near the radio, under the lampshade, are some leaflets which fell from the sky during the last raid. They list the French BBC programs. They also give advice on how to avoid getting caught. Listening to the BBC entails risking high fines, three months of jail and being taken hostage.

alk to the French

La Fayette

The prisonners of Saint Quentin protested until it became a riot. They want to participate in the war effort. According to the "Sun Telegraph". In fact, they wanted better treatment and an opportunity to make a few dollars.
Anyway, it's a sign. Our newpapers talk only of war. From now on, it's on everyone's mind.

Victory gardens

After the disaster of Pearl Harbor, the Americans enter the war on the 7th of December 1941. Still they have some trouble controlling the huge economic movement that they have initiated. The entire country's structure is turned upside down. Sixteen million Americans are enrolled in the Armed Forces. The unemployed rush to military hardware plants. The problem of the treatment of Blacks is increasingly obvious : around one million Afro-Americans are grouped into segregated units of the army. The country is deserted — 20 percent of the rural population leaves the land —, and there is the threat of a labor shortage. To compensate for a down swing in agricultural production, the department of Agriculture launches a "Victory garden" operation. These vegetable gardens are supposed to fill the void provoked by the rush to the factories. Eighteen million vegetable gardens are planted.

We are Here

Depuis le temps que Londres se rine narquoi- sement en parlant du recul des allemands : "C'est la defense élastique", nous commençons à comprendre ce que cela veut dire lorsqu'on trace la ligne de front sur les cartes.

Russie, Normandie et Italie, nous avons trois fronts à mettre à jour tous les matins. Une prouesse !

London has mockingly qualified the Germans' retreat, over and over, as an "elastic defense". This has gone on for so long now that we are starting to understand what it means when we draw the front line on the few maps we can find. Most of the maps have been swept up by the Germans. Russia, Normandy and Italy, we have three fronts to keep up to date every morning. What a feat!

A staff meeting in each house

The French dining room is progressively transforming into a briefing room. Maps of all the fronts are placed on the walls. First these maps must be found, however. This is not easy since after D-Day there is not a single Michelin map left. The Germans have requisitioned them. Anyway those were the maps the Germans used to invade France in 1940. With Russia, things are simple : the small flags have not moved much for a long time. One does not know where to pin them anymore. For the fronts of Normandy and above all of Italy, there is no time to waste. There are many technical problems to solve. The number of flags has increased ; the pins are not solid enough anymore and they bend under the pressure of events. In Autumn 1944 London Radio stops broadcasting. What a pity ! The armchair strategists are completely lost.

Strategy becomes a family pastime : each person feels, within themselves, the soul of an Eisenhower, a Montgomery, a Leclerc or a de Lattre.

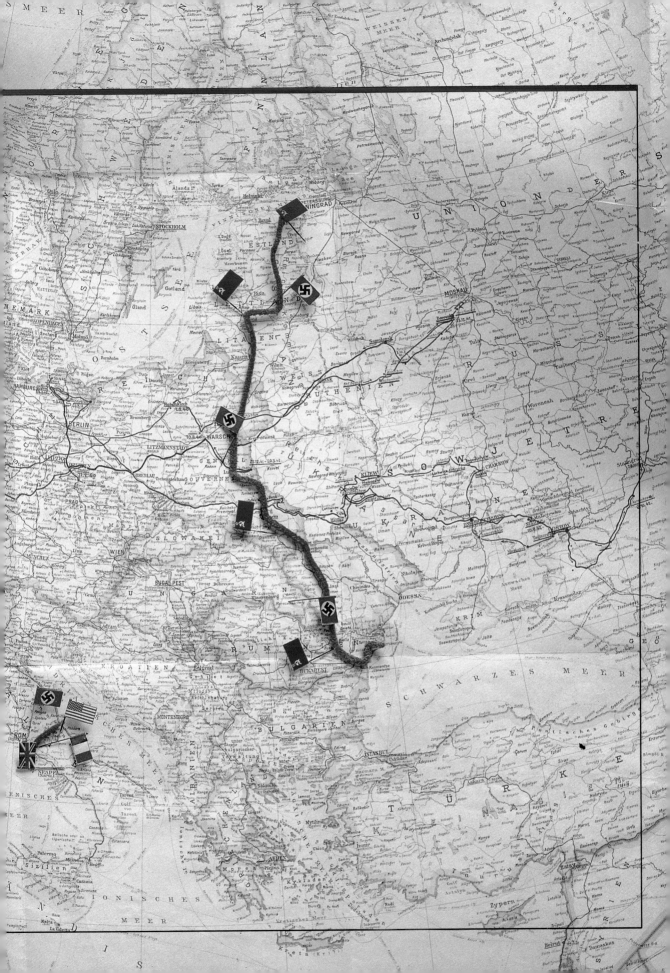

Radio is like chocolate, once you taste it you can't live without it. Radio London is best at night when you are calmer; Radio Sottens at midday is for devotees of René Payot; and Radio Paris during the day gives ten news updates. Jean Herold-Paquis' editorials always end with, "Like Carthage, England..." Foremost is Philippe Henriot: with his convincing golden voice, you have to remind yourself not to trust him.

The press : the Germans' puppet

Convinced of the importance of the press and radio, Dr. Goebbels' specialists organize propaganda in France. No newspaper is published in Paris when they enter the capital; every one of them has retreated to the provinces. Progressively the Germans authorize the republication of *Le Petit Parisien*, *L'Oeuvre* with Marcel Déat and *Paris Soir* (2 million copies in 1939). They facilitate the creation of other titles like *Le Cri du peuple*, *La Gerbe*, *Je suis partout*. All of these newspapers are controlled by the occupying forces, and every day their editors take orders from Goebbels' men. The news information agency is German. The paper supply is controlled by Germans as is distribution. There is extensive censorship; newspapers often appear with entire paragraphs blocked out.

England Will Be Destroyed

The main newspapers like *Paris Soir* withdraw to the Free Zone. Convinced of the importance of the press, the Germans authorize some of them to reappear in the Occupied Zone, but only under their control. In the beginning at least, famous intellectuals and journalists write in the collaborationist newspapers, especially in new ones like *Je suis partout*, *La Gerbe*, *Aujourd'hui* and *Les Nouveaux Temps*. Most of these titles are quickly discredited, however, because of their anti-semitism and their articles full of hatred for Gaullists and Resistance « terrorists. »

Instructions de Bayard pour le sabotage des locos.
Placer les charges sur l'extrémité arrière du cylindre où circule le piston. Toujours celui de droite. Les boches ne peuvent réparer la loco avec celui d'une autre machine endommagée à gauche.
En sabotant toujours du même côté deux machines sont immobilisées à chaque coup —

Bayard ordered us to sabotage the locomotives. We put the charges on the back end of the cylinder where the piston circulates, always the right cylinder. If one always sabotages on the same side, two engines are immobilized at once each time. And there is not a single thing that the Krauts can do about it.

Armbands and badges from the Resistance and the Free French

The army of the "Sans Culotte"

Forces françaises de l'intérieur, Francs tireurs et partisans, soldiers of the Secret Army, fighters of the *Maquis*, members of a clandestine network : the Army of the Shade is a key element in the fight for liberation. Membership varies. In 1943, the STO swells the ranks of the Resistance. Around 20,000 fighters are armed. At the beginning of 1944, there are 40,000, by July 200,000. Numbers remain imprecise and disputed. Their mission : to hamper the efforts of the occupying army as much as possible. Their weapons : whatever London can send them. They share a common faith. The writers Joseph Kessel and Maurice Druon and the musician Anna Marly write *Le Chant des partisans*, which becomes the historical hymn of the French Resistance. At the time of Liberation, *maquis* fighters join the army of de Lattre de Tassigny and the 2nd Armored Division of Leclerc. Those who do not return to civilian life anonymously. More than 100,000 of them will disappear during WW2.

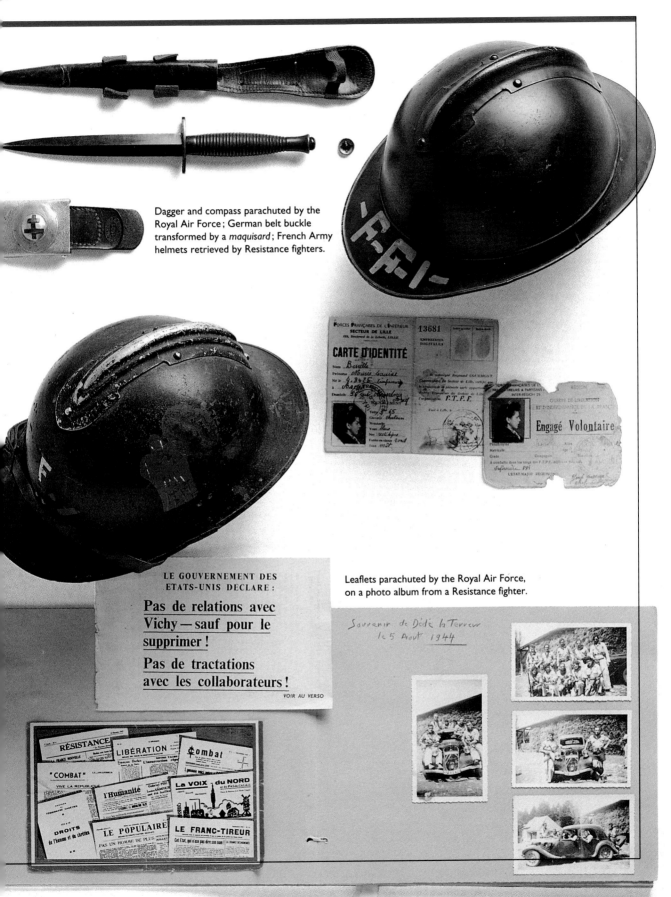

Dagger and compass parachuted by the Royal Air Force; German belt buckle transformed by a *maquisard*; French Army helmets retrieved by Resistance fighters.

Leaflets parachuted by the Royal Air Force, on a photo album from a Resistance fighter.

LE GOUVERNEMENT DES ETATS-UNIS DECLARE :

Pas de relations avec Vichy — sauf pour le supprimer !

Pas de tractations avec les collaborateurs !

VOIR AU VERSO

Souvenir de Dédé la Terreur le 5 Août 1944

Ils arrivent.... Les voilà! Sur la tourelle de leurs chars. Au volant de leurs drôles de petites voitures sans toit. De grands garçons, au sourire épanoui. Le casque négligemment posé de travers sur la tête.
Ils jettent par poignées des cigarettes, du chewing gum et des rations "K".
Tout le monde s'embrasse! Jamais je n'oublierai le délicieux goût de miel de l'été '44!

They came... They are here! On the turret of their tanks. Driving their strange little roofless cars. Big boys... with radiant smiles and helmets carelessly tipped to one side. They throw handfuls of cigarettes, chewing-gum and K-rations. I'll never forget this delicious Summer 1944! Sweet as honey!

Coca Cola floods France

French people are surprised and enchanted by the various varieties of chewing gum (there is even one that tastes like toothpaste), candy, ice cream, K-rations (a day's supply of dehydrated food in a very compact form), Coca Cola, nylon stockings and... cigarettes.

If American cigarettes abound during the Liberation days, they quickly become rarer and rarer. For a long period they can be found only on the black market. Their new taste pleasantly replaces the smell of the *Gauloise* shag, of mixtures like artemisia and dried rose petals, all of which people have smoked over four years.

CHOCOLATE IS A *Fighting* FOOD !

MAXIMUM nourishment with minimum bulk has been the objective of the U. S. Army in selecting the food for our fighting men.

That is why the chocolate bar has come into its own on every fighting front of the war. For there is more quick energy packed into the familiar chocolate bar than is contained in many recommended energy foods. It has become one of the answers to the problem of keeping the soldier supplied with food in modern, high-speed, mobile warfare.

In fact, today the important Type D Army Emergency Ration for use under extreme field conditions is a chocolate bar.

Delicious, nutritious and compact—chocolate is everybody's favorite, whether on the fighting front as an energy food, or on the home front as a quick pick-me-up.

Although serving our fighting men comes first, Nestlé's Chocolate Bars in the familiar Nestlé's wrappers, may still be found on dealers' shelves throughout the country.

COMPARATIVE *ENERGY* VALUES

		Calories
NESTLÉ	1 5¢ Bar Nestlé's Milk Chocolate	217
	1 Medium Lamb Chop (Broiled)	178
	1 Glass Milk (8 oz.)	169
	2 Eggs	140
	2 Slices Bread	200

A 5¢ bar of Nestlé's Milk Chocolate gives you approximately one-tenth the minimum daily requirement for an adult in calcium, phosphorus and iron.

The famous Toll House Cookies can be made only with Nestlé's Semi-Sweet Chocolate.

Nestlé's Chocolate with or without Almonds and Nestlé's Crunch.

A blend of choice cocoa and pure whole milk—already sweetened. Made in a jiffy.

NESTLÉ'S THE WORLD'S GREATEST NAME IN CHOCOLATE

Breakfast RATION TYPE K
Open inner bag carefully. It may be used as a waterproof container for matches, cigarettes and other items. For security, hide the empty can and wrappers so that they cannot be seen.

Dinner RATION TYPE K
Open inner bag carefully. It may be used as a waterproof container for matches, cigarettes and other items. For security, hide the empty can and wrappers so that they cannot be seen.

Supper RATION TYPE K
Open inner bag carefully. It may be used as a waterproof container for matches, cigarettes and other items. For security, hide the empty can and wrappers so that they cannot be seen.

Coca-Cola never managed to become popular in France until the American troops arrived. The famous fizzy drink has maintained its popularity ever since.

A superb discovery for women : nylon stockings that run less easily and have no seam. The fact that they are artificial gives them a lot of added prestige. Every woman dreams of having a pair, but it is not easy.

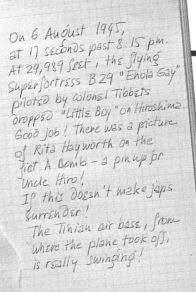

On 6 August 1945, at 17 seconds past 8:15 p.m. At 29,989 feet, the flying Superfortress B 29 "Enola Gay" piloted by Colonel Tibbets dropped "Little Boy" on Hiroshima. Good job! There was a picture of Rita Hayworth on the first A. Bomb – a pinup for Uncle Hiro!
If this doesn't make Japs surrender!
The Tinian air base, from where the plane took off, is really swinging!

A morale booster

With their long legs, their impeccable figures and their suggestive négligées, pin-ups do more for GI morale than do victory bulletins from General Headquarters. Photographed for *Yank* or drawn by Varga in *Esquire*, they are on the front line to cure homesick boys. Pinups, chewing-gum and Virginia cigarettes are considered part of an American soldier's equipment.

Pinups can be found everywhere. Under tents, in GI barracks, on calendars, on writing paper. Not to mention those more or less skillfully painted on the fuselage of the bombers. They insure that the bombs are dropped with "softness and love."

But in the United States feminist leagues petition the government to ban pinups for provocation of "perverse thoughts."

...ead the Ball

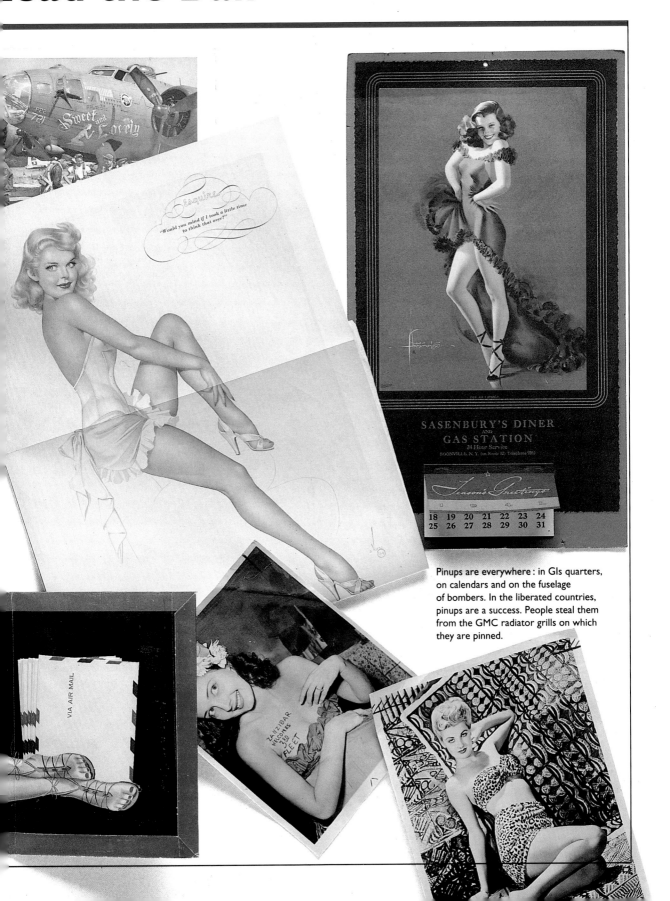

SASENBURY'S DINER
AND
GAS STATION
24-Hour Service
BOONVILLE, N. Y. (on Route 12) Telephone 7212

Season's Greetings

| 18 | 19 | 20 | 21 | 22 | 23 | 24 |
| 25 | 26 | 27 | 28 | 29 | 30 | 31 |

Pinups are everywhere : in GIs quarters,
on calendars and on the fuselage
of bombers. In the liberated countries,
pinups are a success. People steal them
from the GMC radiator grills on which
they are pinned.

Yesterday, my wife and I
saw "Mrs Minniver".
The minister's service in
a church torn apart by
German bombs was deeply
moving. Greek Garson was
marvellous, as usual!
We've never known bombings
in America.
Thank goodness, the English
are fighting back.
We have waited far too long
to participate in this war.

Gone with the history

Anglo-Saxon culture fascinates the French. They can only find classic literature, however, because contemporary English and American books have been banned. Nevertheless, many French people read the big successes of 1939 as well as Somerset Maugham, George Blake, but only procured through the "black market." The curtain falls entirely on cultural information from across the Atlantic. Best-sellers like *The Keys of the Kingdom* and *For Whom the Bell Tolls* are unknown. The same goes for the music of Bartok, Milhaud and Stravinski who enjoy huge success in the United States. In jazz, Duke Ellington, Benny Goodman and Glenn Miller triumph. Frank Sinatra and Bing Crosby are in a field of their own. Those in Europe must wait for peace to bring them *Citizen Kane*, *Casablanca*, *Mrs. Miniver* or *Henry V*. Chaplin films are similarly delayed. Unable to export, Walt Disney Studios switches over to production of military films. Exported to France through GIs, the boogie-woogie is wildly popular and people dance to *Tico Tico* for a long time to come.

Many of the characters that appeared in the fo are still popular today.

BOMBS AWAY
THE STORY OF A BOMBER TEAM
Written for the U. S. Army Air Forces
BY JOHN STEINBECK

With Photographs by

Movie stars exchange
their costumes
for uniforms.

JAMES M. CAIN

Erskine Caldwell

SINCLAIR LEWIS

JOHN STEINBECK
LÂCHEZ
LES BOMBES!

J. C. FURNAS
HOW
AMERICA LIVES

Deadline at Dawn
ARMED SERVICES EDITION
THIS IS THE COMPLETE BOOK. NOT A DIGEST.

The GI « pocketbook ».

Literature (American paperback books in English and in
French), jazz (Victory records and giant records for
radio broadcasts) follow the American troops.
Artists come to perform for the GIs. (Lena Horne,
shown here, is the unforgettable singer of *Stormy
Weather*.)

MOVIE diary

Lovely Day Tomorrow
ORDS & MUSIC BY
VING BERLIN

WAR DEPARTMENT
THE ARMED FORCES RADIO SERVICE

Voxx
No. 126B
GOOD FOR NOTHIN' JOE
Lena Horne with Cab Calloway
or his Orchestra
Vocal

> England is occupied — not Europe! How annoying to see the French Kepis everywhere, the sailors' red pompoms and the big pie-shaped berets of the alpine "chasseurs." That's what comes of having alps! They talk at the top of their voices and take our pubs by storm. I'll be glad when the British have won the war and we are on our own again!

Bachi (sailor's cap), office cap, badges and flag of th FNFL (*Forces navales françaises libres*, the Free French Navy); green ber from the 1st Battalion of Marines Commando (19 jacket and black beret o Special Air Service; paratrooper badges and wings.

Present at the call

Adventurers who go to London often become the soldiers of the FFL. They have all sorts of uniforms and badges : the sailor's hat, the officer's cap of the British Royal Navy, the pilot's wings, the anchor of the French Colonial Army. They also often have the uniform of the Tommies or the "smock" of the Special Air Service paratroopers with the word France written on their sleeve. Simply because they go to the wrong recruiting office, they end up in the British army. Everybody recruits in London. Among the FFL, there are French military personnel or civilians from the colonies who join General de Gaulle. It is a real choice that each one must make, especially the sailors who are far away from France. They can return to their half-occupied country or join the Allied forces. Mostly they prefer to live free or die.

EN AFRIQUE
EN FRANCE
PARTOUT

UN SEUL COMBAT
POUR UNE SEULE PATRIE

Printed by "The Sun Process Engraving Co. Ltd." Manchester, for the "Free French."

Medal ribbons, badges, certificates, jacket and cap of pilots from the FAFL (*Forces aériennes françaises libres*, The Free French Air Force).

F.N.F.L.

FRANCE

FRANCE

FRANCE

The New Arm

Nous voilà dans la Première Armée de De Lattre -
On ne peut pas dire qu'on y est bien reçus. Malgré les discours.
Nous avons tout gardé : nos traditions, comme dit le Colon, mais aussi nos vieux fusils. Mêmes nos vieilles pompes qui prennent la flotte !
Les autres soldats — les vrais — sont sapés et armés par les ricains -
On est des demi-soldats quoi !
Heureusement on reste entre nous.

We belong to De Lattre's 1st Army at last. We can't say we've been well received though, regardless of the speeches. We have kept our traditions, as the colonel says, yes, but everything else too : our old rifles, even our old shoes which leak. The other soldiers, the "real" ones, are dressed and armed by the Yanks. Are we half-soldiers, or what? Hopefully we will stick together.

The volunteers of 1940

The 1st French Army includes the French, the North Africans and elements of the legendary French Colonial Army. Named de Lattre's Army, after its general, it lands on the coasts of Provence on the 16th of August 1944. Less than a month later, on the 11th of September, north of Dijon, de Lattre joins Patton, who arrives from Normandy. On its way, the 1st Army recruits the FFI groups who want to continue fighting. They number 87,000 men by December. The traditional officers of the army do not appreciate the leaders of these "gangs" that sport numerous stripes – often upside down. The FFI continue the struggle with equal ardor, and arrive at the appointed date on the banks of the Danube river. By becoming soldiers, the *maquisards* enter history for the second time.

Left : insignia : 1. 1st Shock Battalion ; 2. 3rd Algerian Infantry Regiment and 3rd Moroccan Spahis Regiment ; 3. 1st Chasseurs-Paratroopers Regiment ; 4. French Commando (4th I.R.; Cluny) ; 5. 1st Marine Battalion ; 6. 1st Marine Regiment ; 7. 2nd Dragoon Regiment ; 8. 1st Free French Division ; 9. French Task Force in Italy ; 10, 11. 1st French Army ; 12. 13th Half-Brigade of the Foreign Legion ; 13. March Regiment of the Foreign Legion.

Has Arrived

Cap from the 13th HBFL, helmet from the 3rd MSR and jumping helmet of the 1st Chasseurs-paratroopers Regiment.

Pennants from the 4th Brigade of the 1st Free French Division; the 3rd Algerian Infantry Division; and the 13th HBFL.

TCHAD

RHIN

LA VICTOIRE DE COLMAR

20 JANVIER - 9 FÉVRIER 1945

A PARIS

ÉDITIONS D'HISTOIRE ET D'ART
LIBRAIRIE PLON

LIBÉRATION DE L'ALSACE

1ᵉʳ ARMÉE FRANÇAISE
«RHIN ET DANUBE»

BRAUN & CIE

Le TROISIEME RÉGIMENT DE
TIRAILLEURS ALGÉRIENS
EN ITALIE
JANVIER-AOÛT 1944

LES ÉDITIONS DE LA NOUVELLE FRANCE

J'ai téléphoné dans plusieurs banlieues pour savoir où sont les américains.
On les a vus, paraît-il, du côté d'Étampes.
Un bougnat m'a répondu de La Croix de Berny à 10 km de Paris. Ils viennent de passer, des français sur des chars, coiffés d'un calot rouge.
Ils ne sont pas beaucoup. Une avant-garde sans doute. Vive la France!

2nd (French) Armored Division insignia.

Caps for Colonial and Home Troops.

Called several suburbs to find out where the Americans are. Apparently they have been seen near Etampes. The owner of a bar told me that they just passed near La Croix-de-Berny, 6 miles from Paris. Frenchmen with red caps on tanks, and not many either. A vanguard probably. Long live France!

The crazy ride

Twice arrested, Lieutenant Philippe de Hautecloque escapes from France and joins de Gaulle in London in June 1940. There, he is named governor of Cameroon which he wins over to the Free French.

He assumes the name Leclerc in order to protect his family, still in France, from any consequences related to his actions. Commanding the AEF, he penetrates the Libyan desert with a column of soldiers of the Free French Forces and takes the oasis of Kufra from the Italians in March 1941. He vows not to lay down his arms before placing the tricolor flag on Metz and Strasbourg. Leclerc gets a foothold on French soil in western Normandy on the 1st of August 1944. Heading the prestigious 2nd Armored Division, he liberates Paris (which rebels on the 24th of August), and receives the surrender of von Choltitz. Strasbourg is taken by surprise on the 23rd of November, and on the 2nd of May 1945 Leclerc hoists the French flag on Hitler's "eyrie" in Berchtesgaden. An oath carried through to its triumphant end!

Cap, photo and insignia of the 501st Combat Tank Regiment.

The French actor Jean Marais served in the 2nd Armored Division.

Marine M10 tank destroyer (painting by Brenet);
pennant of the Marine Armored Regiment;
pennant of the 12th Armored Cavalry Regiment.

Colonial
infantry cap.

I saw an extraordinary display of medals in a Picadilly shop. Not only British ones, but from all over the world. Polish, Belgian and French "Croix de guerre" and even the "Croix de la Libération", a medal that de Gaulle has just introduced. Not a single "Légion d'honneur" though. The craftsman who weaves the ribbons never stops in his small workshop. For him, this great meeting of world armies in London is excellent business.

United States: Medal of Congress; Silver Star; Bronze Star; Purple Heart; Distinguished Service Cross; Distinguished Service Medal. Army Good Conduct; Distinguished Flying Cross; Air Medal; European Theatre of Operation.

The Liberation takes orders

Among the most important Allied decorations, only the *Légion d'honneur* is not conferred during the war years. Concerned with questions of legality in this field, General de Gaulle is neither willing nor able to attribute this old and prestigious decoration. Because of this and because he wants specific medals for specific circumstances, he creates the Order of the Liberation. It is awarded only to the French who joined him in London, to those who fought in the ranks of the Free French Forces, and to primary Resistance network leaders whom he personally nominated. The *Croix de la Libération* is rarely conferred and then only on a limited number of "companions". To emphasize the significance of this decoration, de Gaulle declares that the Order must include 783 "companions" chosen among the FFL, 107 chosen among the agents of the intelligence networks, 157 from the interior Resistance, 6 women and 14 communists... A true profession of faith.

Great-Britain:

Distinguished Service Order; Victoria Cross; Distinguished Flying Cross; 1939-1945 Star; Aircrew Star; Burma Star; 1939-45 Medal; War Medal.

Only One Address : London

France : Commandeur de la Légion d'honneur.
Officier de la Légion d'honneur ; 2. Médaille de la Résistance ; 3.
Médaille des Evadés ;
Great-Britain : 4. Military Cross ; 5. 1939-45 Star ; 6. Burma Star ; 7.
France and Germany Star ; 8. 1939-45 War Medal.

Lieutenant Robert Sauvage
of the Normandy-Niemen
French-Soviet Squadron,
1945.

Soviet pilot's wings

1 2 3 4 5 6 7 8

France : Croix de la
Libération ; Médaille militaire ;
Croix de Guerre 1939-45 ;
Médaille de la Résistance ;
Campagne d'Italie 1943-44 ;
Commémorative 1939-45 ;
Combattant volontaire
Résistant.

Dutch Flying Cross.
Czech War Cross 1939-45.

USSR : Soviet Union Hero ; Red Flag Order ; Normandy Niemen
Squadron ; Patriotic War Order ; Alexandre Nevsky Order ; Red Star
Order ; Konigsberg Seizure Medal (1945), Victory over Germany.
Red Army identity cards and documents.

We raided a print shop in the middle of the afternoon. No problems. We packed huge reams of paper into our front-wheel drive Citroën. They were so heavy that the exhaust pipe scraped the cobblestones. It's to print Combat. Hanging on the headlamp I perched on the mudguard to cover our retreat while we passed through the town like a whirlwind. Our cargo was transferred to a truck waiting at the edge of the forest.

From Resistance to Liberation

The first newspapers of the French Resistance are individually typed and stenciled, and slipped into letterboxes by small teams as early as 1940. Around 1941 these newspapers are printed in real print shops. Printruns increase quickly. In 1943, the Vichy police announce that 540,000 copies of clandestine newspapers have been seized and destroyed. Some newspapers like *Combat* have several regional editions. Launched by 20-year-old students, *Défense de la France* has a print shop in 1942. It appears twice a month and runs 20,000 copies. By 1944, it has seven print shops. By the Liberation, the "clandestine" press has about a hundred national newspapers and numerous regional and local ones. It includes a total of 2 million copies. Most of these newspapers continue after the Liberation and develop into the major titles of the national press.

he Free Press !

May 8th, 1945

Everybody wears a badge celebrating the victory on their lapel, shirt or blouse. There are badges for all tastes and political tendencies. From the hilarious Tommy to the French rooster – more cock-a-doodle-do than ever – to the Croix de Lorraine.

Many of the leaders are glorified : de Gaulle, Leclerc, Eisenhower, Montgomery, sometimes Churchill, almost never Stalin. All of the badges include a hand with two fingers raised forming the V of Victory.

It was just announced that peace has been signed. All the bells in Paris are ringing. It's extraordinary. What a glorious day! Everybody is in the street, like they were on Liberation day. We have been free for nine months already. Each day we discover something new about this war. What is there still to learn about these years that we'd rather chase from our memories?

Songs of victory

May 8th, 1945 is a torrid day with an unprecedented blue sky. In French towns and villages, bells sound out songs of jubilation instead of the alarm. The victory opens new opportunities. The war is finally over and various scientific discoveries announce the birth of a new and hopefully better world.

The Americans are building a machine that calculates a hundred times faster than a human does. The antibiotics that saved many wounded soldiers are increasingly used to treat civilians. Planes take off and land in all weather. Cars become more and more common. At this moment in history, there seems nothing left that is impossible for mankind. The war brought great leaps in technology, but at what price? Nearly 50 million died, including 25 million civilians and 12 million people in Russia alone.

What a Party!

L'INSURRECTION PARISIENNE
19 août — 1944 — 26 août

Préface de Jacques DUCLOS — PRIX : 10 FRANCS

VIVE LES ALLIÉS

VIVE LES FFI

VM

Vivre libre ou Mourir

20 PHOTOS VÉRITABLES DE LA Libération DE PARIS

...g live the Allies! Long ...freedom! Slogans, ...tos, postcards and ...ers with small Allied ...invade the streets. ...party lasts until ...mer.

Footnotes

AEF (Afrique Equatoriale Française/French Equatorial Africa) : A federation of four African territories under French control between 1910 and 1958. Later became independent (Central African Republic, Congo, Gabon and Chad).

Atlantic Wall : A group of fortified defense works, built between the Netherlands and Biarritz, which was supposed to prevent any landing on the coasts of France.

B17s and B24s : "Flying fortresses," American bombers with a wide range. Used during the last years of the war, specially for important missions over Japan.

Bauleiter : Works manager of the Todt Organization.

BCRA (Bureau central de renseignements et d'action) : De Gaulle's Intelligence organization in London.

Berchtesgaden : Hitler's fortified residence in the Bavarian Alps.

Bevin boys : A name given to the English called upon by Bevin. Bevin was Minister of Labour and of the National Service in Winston Churchill's government and member of the Labour Party.

Blitz : German word for lightning. Intensive all-out aerial attack or campaign. Also period during which Britain endured permanent bombings.

Block leader : One responsible for the Civil Defense of a specific area.

Büros : German administration in charge of buying French raw materials and food for distribution in Germany. They also proceed to requisitions and collect the debts of war. The high prices fixed by the *Büros* stimulate the black market. Still, the occupying forces win out by imposing the rate of exchange of the deutschmark.

Choltitz, Dietrich von (1894-1966) : The military governor of Paris in 1944, who refuses to obey Hitler's orders to dynamite the main bridges and monuments of Paris.

Collabos : Name given by the Resistance fighters to French people who accepted to cooperate with Germany.

Concours Lépine : Inventors competition organized each year in Paris, named after the préfet Lépine who conceived the social event.

Containers : The metal cylinders used to parachute food, medicine and weapons.

Dakota : The English name of the C47VS, the first plane entirely built in metal. These planes are issued in 1935 and 10,650 of them are produced for the American army.

Darlan, François (1881-1942). Admiral who was the vice-president of the Ministers' Council under the Pétain Government after Pierre Laval was removed from office.

Death's heads : The white-metal badges worn on the lapel of the green tunic of the soldiers from German armored divisions (Panzerdivisionen) .

Demarcation line : An arbitrary frontier, set by Hitler after the armistice of 1940, which cuts France into two. The Northern Zone is occupied and the Southern Zone is non-occupied, or free.

Djellabah : A long dress with sleeves and cowl worn by men and women in North Africa.

DSO (Distinguished Service Order) : British medal.

D.Z. (Dropping Zone) : 6,400 m² square parachuting field. Two kinds of planes are used for the pick-up operations (dropping and picking up agents; transporting documents). The Lysander needs 600 yards to land and the Hudson MK1 1,000 yards.

BBC : The British Radio broadcasts information bulletins in French and Dutch every day for the occupied countries. Transmission also reaches Germany where it is much listened to.

Ersatz : A substitutive product replacing one of a better quality.

Exodus : A mass panic which first sends the Belgians and then also the French fleeing on the roads during the German attack of May 1940.

FFI (Forces françaises de l'intérieur) : A structure created on the 1st of February 1944, theoretically regrouping all the military organizations of the French Resistance.

Flak : (from the German *Fliegabwehrkannone*) : anti-aircraft guns.

FTP (Francs-Tireurs et Partisans) : The guerilla organization of the National Front, a predominantly communist Resistance organization.

FW (Focke Wulf) : A German fighter.

Frontstalags : prisoner camps rapidly organized in France.

Gauloise : A famous French cigarettes brand.

GMC : General purpose trucks with six-wheel drive made by General Motors. Used by the Allies, including the Soviets.

Half tracks : armored vehicles which transport Allied soldiers to the battlefield. 50,000 will be produced.

Halifax : Heavy English bomber used for dropping bombs and parachuting equipment. It can carry up to 9 tons of cargo, and fly at less than one hundred meters from the ground at a speed of 180 km/h. All these planes belong to the "black squadrons." They are named "black squadrons", for security reasons, they fly by moonless nights and are painted black.

Henriot, Philippe (1899-1944) : Right-wing Deputy, one of the leaders of the *Milice*, secretary of State at the Department of Information and Propaganda under the Vichy

régime. Contributing editor for Radio Paris, was shot by the Resistance.

Herold-Paquis, Jean : Aggressive anti-British a anti-American journalist at Radio-Paris.

HQ : Headquarters.

Hurricane : An English fighter which plays important role in the Battle of Britain.

Ike : General Eisenhower's nickname.

IS : Intelligence Service.

Jeep : Named by the initials of "GP" (Gene Purpose) and after a little cartoon character. diminutive motor vehicle of 1/4 ton capac equipped with four wheel-drive during WV The Willys Overland Company had alrea started production in 1939 and went on produce millions of vehicles.

Jerries : One of the many derogatory nicknam for the Germans. Other examples include : Hu Boches and Krauts.

Jerrycan or jerrican : name given to a 5-gal container used by the Germans to carry gas.

Je suis partout (I Am Everywhere) : Founded 1930, this royalist weekly turned pro-fascist collaborationist. It was notably anti-semitic a had signatures of many famous writers.

K-ration : A ration allotted to the Ameri soldiers, supplying food for a whole day in a v compact form.

Kommandantur : The German command p for a region or town.

Kufra : An oasis in Libya.

Lancaster : An English bomber, which transpc powerful bombs nicknamed "Tallboy" and " Slam" (10,900 pounds and 18,000 pounds).

de Lattre de Tassigny (1889-1952) : The gene in charge of the 1st French Army, embryo of New Army.

Légion d'honneur (Legion of Honor) : T decoration is conferred by the Order headec a Main Chancellor who is named by the Vi government. Because of this, General de Gaul absolutely unable to give such a decoration.

Liberty ships : Mass-produced by the Americ they replaced the numerous cargo ships sunk German submarines during the Atlantic ba They transported men and material for the Al

Luftwaffe : The German Air Force.

LVF (Légion des volontaires français) : T French Legion of Volunteers fighting for Gern on the Russian front.

Mae West : A yellow inflatable life jacket wor fliers and named after an American actress wi notably full figure.

Maquis and maquisard : French Resista (*Maquis*) named after the bush where Resistance fighters (*maquisards*) hide.

(Messerschmitt): A German fighter plane.
: last model of which – the ME263 – is
pelled by turbojets. It flies at 900 km/h and
: all the Allied fighters in its time. Fortunately,
as not produced in sufficient quantities to
ence the course of the war.

n Kampf (My Struggle): Autobiography and
phlet written in 1924 while Hitler was in jail.

tärbefehlshaber: Military commander.

ce: A paramilitary organization which was
ted by the Vichy government to support its
n actions and actively cooperated with
pying forces.

squito: An English plane notably in charge of
g photos.

ty: The nickname for Bernard Montgomery
37-1976) an English Marshal whose strategy
criticized by the Americans.

ional revolution: The Vichy regime pretend-
o free France from the old demons which it
ned had led the country to the disaster of
0: parliamentarism, skepticism and
chialism.

: The Office of Strategic Service: America's
cipal espionage organization during World
II. Its successor – the CIA – came into
ence in 1947.

ser Zeitung (Parisian Newspaper): The title
German newspaper published in French.

ive Defense: A civilian organization respon-
for the application of the orders relating to
ert.

on, George (1885-1945): An American
ral noted for his dynamism and tremendous
.

in, Philippe (1856-1951): General in 1914,
articipates in the battle of Verdun in 1916,
ng which French soldiers stand against a
derous German offensive. Later he wins the
of victor of Verdun because after this battle
French Army is able to launch several
nter-offensives. In 1917, he sucessfully
esses several mutinies in the French Army.
ster of Defense in 1934, French ambassador
pain, he becomes vice-president and then
dent of the Ministers' Council in June 1940.
meets Hitler in Montoire in October 1940
decides to establish a dictatorial State which
orts the Nazis and to fully cooperate with
, including in the prosecution of Jews. He is
ed by a French court in 1945, condemned to
h and then to a life sentence. Dies in jail.

ol: A handgun fed by cartridges set in a clip
ed in the grip.

W: Prisoner of War.

pagandastaffel: German propaganda
nization in France.

o Sottens: A Swiss radio program which
le listened to for René Payot's editorials.

Recruitment: Everybody recruited in London,
the English as well as the French. The trick was to
know the right address.

Relief: system under which, at least in theory,
one French war prisoner would be released if
three skilled workers went to work in Germany.

Rommel's asparagus, lion's teeth: Posts or saw-
horses set in the sand to prevent the landing craft
from getting near the coast.

Royan and Falaise were among several towns
which remained in the hands of the Germans for
a long time after the Normandy landing. Instead
of liberating these areas in which the Germans
fiercely resisted, the Allies bypassed them to
avoid slowing down their advance.

S-Phone: transmission device. Enables talk
between the ground and the crew of the plane
by wireless telegraph. Also facilitates the
technique of landing by helping the pilot land in
line with the field.

Secours national: An organization created by the
Vichy government to help the most destitute. It
distributed clothes, money and food through
local relief services.

Secret Army: includes the military sections of
various French Resistance movements which later
will be merged into the French Forces of the
Interior (FFI).

Semi-automatic: A weapon which only shoots
by volleys although its magazine is automatically
fed.

Sherman: A tank named after the famous
general of the Confederate Army during the
American Civil War.

Ship: A name given by American pilots to heavy
bombers.

Smock: A British paratroopers' jacket.

SOE (Special Organization Executive): A British
war-time organization answering strictly to
Churchill.

Spahis: French Cavalry Regiment created in the
19th century and including North African riders.
Most Spahi Regiments were transformed into
armored units during the Second World War.

Spitfire: A modern British fighter plane which
plays a very important role in the Battle of Britain.

Squadron: formation of fighters or bombers.

Stens: Light British submachine guns parachuted
to the Resistance, and also used by British
soldiers.

STO (Service du Travail Obligatoire): The
compulsory labor service in Germany.

TCRP (Transports en commun de la région
parisienne): The transport authority for metro
and buses in Paris and its suburbs.

Territorial forces: A reserve of the Passive
Defense enlisting men too old to be drafted in
the regular army.

Tinian: An American air base located in the
Mariana Islands in the Pacific Ocean.

Todt, Fritz (1891-1942): The Minister of
Armament and the director of an engineering
service which built 2,500 miles of motorways
before 1938 and many defense works first in
Germany and then in the occupied territories.

TSF (Télégraphie sans fil): The name given to the
first radio receiver sets.

Twenty-five francs: This represents approximately 12.50 francs today, that is 2 US dollars or 1.50
British pounds.

Uderzo, Albert: famous author of comics.
Created the character of Asterix with René
Goscinny.

Vichy: town where the collaborationist
government of Pétain (1940-1944) settled after
the armistice of June 1940. The Vichy government gives all power to Marshal Pétain. Like
Hitler, Franco and Mussolini, Pétain is hostile to
democracy, parliamentarism and the Republican
regime. The government bans all trade unions
and left-wing political parties. Imitating the Nazi
laws of Nuremberg, the Vichy government
obliges the Jews to wear a yellow star; it forbids
them to work as professionals (lawyers, doctors)
and government officials, to own businesses, etc.,
and then arrests the Jews in massive numbers for
deportation to Germany.

V1, V2, V3: "Secret weapons." V is the initial for
Vergeltunswaffe (reprisal weapon). Already used
in 1943, the V1 is a flying bomb with 1,000
pounds of explosives. It causes a lot of damage in
London. The V2, with 2,000 pounds of
explosives, is a true rocket. V1s and V2s take off
from launchers located in the bunkers of Belgium,
Netherlands and northern France. On the 6th of
September 1944, the first V2 launched on Paris
fails. On September 8th, London and Antwerp
are the targets. The V3 is a very long range gun
which remained a prototype. It is estimated that
the Germans are ten years ahead of the Allies in
the field of jet planes, rockets and missiles.

Waffen SS: Elite troups of the German Army
whose exactions bathe the occupied countries in
blood, even more so after the Normandy
landing.

Wehrmacht: The German armed forces.

Youth Workcamps (Chantiers de la jeunesse): A
paramilitary organization of the Vichy government. In the beginning the Youth Workcamps
enroll 100,000 men aged 20 who could have
been but were not drafted in 1940. They settle in
the countryside. These draftees work in the fields
or make the charcoal necessary for cars equipped
with a gas producer. The Workcamps advocate a
"virile Pétainism." Some of those recruited in the
Workcamps later joined the Resistance.

Zazou: An onomatopoeia which punctuates
swing music.

Acknowledgements

We would like to thank all the private individuals and institutions, collectors and museums, who kindly lent us the documents and other items reproduced in this book.

Jean Baillais
Denis Barbe, Conservateur du Musée 1939-1945 à Ambleteuse
Philippe Bartlett
Pierre Besnard
Gérard Blanchard
Jean Bouchery
Serge Bromberg (Lobster Films)
Les Cafés Brasilia
Odile Calvet-Richet
Anne Capet-Proust
Jo Carasso
Marie-Thérèse Chailley
Philippe Charbonnier
Gilles Comte
Didier Corbonnois
Jeanne Damamme, Conservateur du Musée du Jouet à Poissy
Jean-Pierre Dauphin
Jean-Louis d'Elia
Robert d'Elia
Christophe Deschodt, Conservateur du Musée 1939-1945 à Ambleteuse
Philippe d'Hugues
Eve Duperray, Conservateur du Musée de la Résistance à Fontaine-de-Vaucluse
Editions musicales Durand
Jean-Jacques Estella
Pascal Fouché
Cécile Gougat
Gilbert Guez
Fanny Guillon-Laffaille
Hervé Halfen
Xavier Henriot
Joël Hérisson
Eric Hernandez
Jacqueline Heuclin
Richard Ingram
Christian Jambro
Marc Jammet
Régis Jérôme
Danièle Jolly
Pierre Jonquières
Joubert S.A.
Aliette de Lataillade

Eric Lefèvre
Rémy Longetti
Librairie Lutèce 2
Etienne Mangeon
Etablissements Maratier
(location d'armes et costumes)
Jean-Philippe Martinet
Claude Martini
Bernard Massot
Claude Moliterni
Jean-Yves Nasse
Martine Pfeiffer
Jacques Poirier
Marie-Claire Prin
Carmen Raoux-Granier
Julia Salmon-Finel
Marie-Louise Schefer
Patrick Seguy
Peter Sourian
Yves Tariel
Restaurant le Temps des Cerises
Rémy Theis
Titus
Christian Tollet
Jean Toupance
Thierry Valin
Luc Van Malderen

Jean Oberlé, Henri Amouroux, Pierre Miquel, Henri Michel, Claude Dadid, W.L. Shirer, Robert O. Paxton, Anthony Cave Brown, Fred Kupferman, Stéphane Marchetti, René Alleau, Laurent Gervereau, John Campbell, Marc Leproux, Dominique Veillon, Dominique Decèze, Georges Bernage, André Figueras, Myrone N. Cuich, Hervé Le Boterf, Jean Defrasne, Gilles Ragache, Jean-Robert Ragache, Pierre Lorain.

have inspired some of the facts and anecdotes recounted in the diaries.

Musée d'Histoire 1939-1945
L'appel de la liberté
Chemin du Gouffre
84800 Fontaine-de-Vaucluse
Tél. 90 20 24 00.

Musée du Jouet
2, enclos de l'Abbaye
78300 Poissy
Tél. 39 65 06 06
Ouvert du mercredi au dimanche de 9 h 30 à 12 h et de 14 h à 17 h 30. Fermé les jours fériés.

Magasin Overlord
Frédéric Finel
Militaria 1939-1945
6, rue Charles V
75004 Paris
Tél. 42 77 74 47
Ouvert du mardi au samedi de 10 h à 12 h et de 14 h à 19 h 30.

Musée 1939-1945
62164 Ambleteuse
Tél. 21 87 33 01
Ouvert du 1.04 au 15.10 de 9 h 30 à 19 h
800 m² d'exposition, 80 mannequins équipés, salle vidéo.

Assistant Editor :
Nathalie Lemaire.
Computer lay-out and typesetting :
Christian Millet
Concept and design :
Atelier Gérard Finel et Associés.
3, rue Lacépède
75005 Paris
Tél. 43 37 96 16

Printed in Luçon (France) by Pollina S.A. in March 1994.
ISBN : 2 7373 1498 X
N° d'éditeur : 2 88801 040494